Edited by Trevor [illegible]

The publisher gratefully acknowledges all the individuals who granted Hope Pages Press Ltd. First print rights. All copyrights of the contained stories remain with their individual authors.

First paperback edition January 2022

Cover art, logo & book design by Michael Arendt
Edited & compiled by Trevor Ritchie & Michael Arendt

Paperback: ISBN 978-1-7775688-0-1
E-book: ISBN 978-1-7775688-1-8

www.hopepagespress.com

Table of Contents

Acknowledgements

Putting together this anthology has been a labour of love, and it's been through the dedicated work and actions of many different people that you have this book in your hands today.

First, and absolutely foremost, we want to give our sincere thanks to Ryan Clayton, whose brainchild this anthology was and who continues to support the publication and sharing of queer stories.

A special note of appreciation to our coworkers, who have watched us balance our careers and the needs of Alphabet of Hope to reach publication on time and with the best quality product we could possibly create.

Any set of acknowledgments that doesn't include our wonderful authors would be incomplete, so we want to thank the individuals who submitted their stories for this anthology. Your strength and willingness to share parts of yourselves with the rest of the world is an inspiration.

Finally, we want to acknowledge you as the reader of this anthology. This book is for you. We hope that you'll find comfort and inspiration from the stories you read and see there are many different ways to live your life. More than comfort and inspiration, we hope this book fills you with hope. Hope for yourself, hope for your communities, hope for the society you live in.

A Letter to My Past Self

Written by Lillith Campos

I wrote this to myself July 2nd of 2019. This was in the days leading up to my name change. My therapist had suggested some kind of ceremony, something to commemorate my name change. I had struggled with wanting to do something for this milestone in my life. I had socially transitioned 3 weeks prior, and I really wanted to celebrate my transition somehow. My days as Greg were numbered and I wanted closure on that chapter in my life. In the 2 years seeing my therapist exploring my gender I would 'write' in a diary on my phone and let my therapist read it at the beginning of each session and that would dictate how the session would go. I had showed an affinity for expressing myself through writing in the previous 2 years so writing me a letter from him to her was my assignment. This would be the very first of my essays about my transition and what we as transgender people go through.

Lillith,

Take a breath. Look down at your two feet. Where are they right now? Look around you. Do you see nature? Go touch the leaves. Pick a flower and deeply inhale its beautiful fragrance. Do you hear birds? Stop and take a moment to go listen to their music, because not everyone is so fortunate enough to be able to hear and enjoy that experience. Do you feel the sunshine on your skin? If not, go step outside and be grateful for the fact that it is constantly shining down on you, and that you are alive.

Life isn't a sprint, it's a long race and you're not in it just to "win." Be gentle with yourself. Be messy sometimes. Let it all go. Embrace all of your learnings and cherish your experiences because they truly are divinely fated.

No one lives forever so be sure to cherish every moment, and when they pass and when you pass, find comfort in knowing that we are simply souls within these bodies, and we will all be connected at some point again. Life is a gift, not something that is a given, so enjoy every second while you're here. Make the most of it. Live it to your fullest and please, be true to yourself Lillie. You had a rough road to travel just to even exist. You are valid, you are real. It's not a dream anymore. I'm handing over the keys to this vessel I've called home for so long. Now it's your turn. I'm sorry it took me so long to realize this was your home and you were screaming to be let in. I know you'll do great things and I know you're truly on your path to happiness now.

While I know you aren't as experienced in the world, you are getting ready. Soon, I'll leave full charge to you, because you are the only one who is truly deserving of this body. Even if it never matches how you feel some days, it will always be yours. I'm sorry for having contaminated it with the presence that was male. My stoic demeanor has been wearing us down, and while it has been partly to hide the pain, it's just as much because of my embarrassment from having you inside. This is your body, not mine. I really hope that I didn't screw it up too much for you. Wear what clothes you want because you deserve to wear them. Be the woman you were destined to be. Don't be defined by my mistakes.

Alphabet of Hope

Years ago, I prayed to anyone and anything that would listen for your happiness. On your road ahead please don't lose hope. We were put here on this earth to feel joy and not be blue. There will be sad times and bad times and I know that you have the strength to see them through. Look at how far you have come. Look at all you've accomplished. Hold your head high! Though I can't know for sure how things will work out for you, no matter how hard it gets, please realize, please understand that you weren't put on this earth to suffer and cry. We were made for being happy. So, for me.... for you.... please.... be happy.

Gregory

Blue Skies
Written By Derek Smith

Lying there in a tatty, old hammock, I felt both a sense of relaxation and nerves as I waited for the go-ahead to board the plane. In 2017, it was at this private airport when I let my guard down and did something that would change so much about myself. For the first time, I allowed someone in who would grab me by the straps, open a door, and throw me out into a new world I had never seen. It would reveal a part of myself I never knew existed and started a chain of events that changed things in ways I couldn't foresee. I had returned to celebrate a milestone I had reached with a flight two years in the making.

I had arrived here in Pemberton, BC, two days before. Still, my celebratory flight kept getting delayed, if not due to weather, then by other passengers bumping me off the queue. I was not a priority, and I didn't let it get to me – I got used to this growing up. But today was going to be the day. There were clear, blue skies, and the winds were calm. I just had to wait my turn. And so I laid there, rocking back and forth in the same hammock I laid down in two years ago, soaking up the sunshine, reflecting on life, and how much I had grown.

Growing up in the '80s and '90s was not particularly difficult for me. Although far from the most popular kid in elementary school, I wasn't the least popular. While I had trouble making friends, I was satisfied with the few friends I had. Sitting comfortably and safely in my little corner, I would watch my classmates grow their circle of friends. I liked it this way as I got little attention.

As a child, I seemed to have a propensity to make myself look like a fool at anything I tried to set my mind to. The other kids would laugh, and I would want to start crying. But I had a defense mechanism at hand! I would simply not try anything new. When I did, I'd keep myself hidden in my corner so no one could see me fail. This strategy worked beautifully in the short term; unfortunately, this only reinforced my social awkwardness.

By the time I entered high school, I had built myself the reputation of being pretty average at everything. I was the last to be chosen for the team in PE; never the first pick for class projects; constantly assigned a partner by the teacher rather than chosen by a classmate. I did such a good job hiding that no one saw my faults, failures, or accomplishments, so there was little reason to select me.

It wasn't until the middle of grade 11 that my sexuality began to reveal itself to me. Frightening without a doubt and with apt skill, I tossed it to the side. Regular social settings were already difficult for me. I couldn't be bothered to deal with something as complicated as my sexuality. Boyfriends and girlfriends were equally foreign concepts to me, and I had little desire for either. Besides, unless you wanted to get beaten up at school, you would never come out as gay.

Through the rest of high school and university, I found it was easier to be average, or at least appear that way, and I nailed that very well. My energy was focused on staying hidden and not exploring myself. The ease of keeping to myself and being unseen by all was intoxicating. I was building myself a room that I felt safe in, protected from society's judgment and hidden from the risks of life. It made life easy.

My sexuality only reinforced my fear of meeting new people and taking chances. But it was getting more challenging to set aside my feelings and deny the fact I was gay. So I accepted my sexuality, and reinforced my room and allowed even fewer people in. I did this through university, getting trapped in a cycle that would leave my social development stagnant. I would depart with only my Master of Science degree; I did not forge a single new friendship. Yet I felt happy, under the illusion life was perfect. I still wasn't out.

The next nine years were a blur of boredom. I would live my so-called perfect life doing what was expected of me. I got an excellent job as a chemist at the University of British Columbia, stayed healthy through my curling, and kept to myself in the background. I hid my sexuality from almost everyone and never took the time to explore myself and truly live. Those who knew me would likely describe me as a shy, quiet, 35-year-old guy steadily going through life. That was accurate. I was all of those.

As far as I was concerned, there was nothing that needed to change. Well, that was wrong. I had trapped myself in this prison that I had been building since my childhood. How do you break out of prison so well constructed you don't even realize you are in it? I was soon to find out some stranger might come and rip you out.

Health was important to me, and I would frequent the gym to stay fit. Early on a Monday morning in May, one of the trainers at my gym approached me. He wanted me to join him and twelve people in Pemberton, enjoy some fun and games, a BBQ, camp overnight, and then go tandem skydiving the next day. He lost me at "twelve people". A social event with people I didn't know was frightening enough, but the thought of jumping out of an airplane was out of the question. Using a few choice words, I declined, telling him to have a good time without me.

But he refused my answer and got other trainers and gym members to pressure me. As I continued to refuse this foolish idea, the pressure mounted. My insistence on refusing to do this insane joyride only seemed to fuel everyone's determination to convince me otherwise. I felt like I was back in elementary school again, being pressured by classmates to take part. So to make it stop, I succumbed to their pressure.

That June, I would put my sleeping bag and backpack in my car, get in, take a deep breath, and begin the drive up to Pemberton to face my fears or die trying. I was going to socialize with strangers. Partaking in such a large event with so many people was intimidating and terrifying. I tried not to even think of skydiving, which was equally terrifying.

I felt so out of place, literally knowing no one other than the trainer organizing it, and I did not know him all that well. Everyone was socializing, splashing around in the pool, playing with the slackline or soccer ball, while I stayed to myself on the patio corner drinking a beer. It was just as if I was back in high school, less the beer!

At our BBQ dinner, considering what we were about to do the next day, I raised a glass to "The Last Supper", much to everyone's horror and amusement. At sunset, I took refuge in the solitude of my tent, mentally exhausted from the day's events.

The next day I woke up to face my fear of heights and thrill rides and perhaps literally die trying. After arriving at the airport and signing my life away, I laid down in their hammock to wait for the weather to improve while everyone else played Spikeball.

Eventually, the weather improved, and Steve strapped another gym member and me into our harnesses and gave us the training briefing. I think Steve could tell how scared I was and was very reassuring. He and everyone else was cheering, and encouraging me, which was a novel experience. No one ever did that for me before. I was not sure how to deal with it and tried my best to enjoy things.

The views of the mountains from the plane were breathtaking. The Cessna had all its seats removed, but for the pilot seat, and windows were everywhere, providing a 360-degree view of the scenery. I was so anxious. The last time I felt so uneasy was my first kiss with a guy. Little did I know my perspective on myself and life was moments from being shattered.

Suddenly I felt the plane levelling off, and the door flipped open, letting in the cold, freezing air into the aircraft. Why did I ever agree to do this? I could have said no and switched gyms to avoid embarrassment. I could have turned right at the highway and driven back home. I could have refused to pay! Clearly, I wasn't thinking straight.

The plane shook as my fellow gym member left the plane first. My heart was beating like mad.

Strapped tightly onto Steve, I was dragged to the open door and quickly found my feet dangling outside. I felt the cold wind against the side of my head as I made the mistake of looking out the open door and down below. Steve pushed my forehead back, and I felt my body rocking. The air slammed into my face, faster and faster, and a world I didn't know was there came rushing towards me.

As we fell, the sheer terror in my face – well captured by Steve's hand camera – changed into adrenaline-filled excitement. During the entire fall from leaving the plane to reaching the ground, everything frightening about life, and indeed myself, was gone. For the first time, I was living in the moment. I had never felt this feeling before. I wanted more.

What the Hell is wrong with me? I want to do that again!? What a terrifying thought. Who is this voice speaking into my mind?

The part of myself holding me back in life was left on that plane that summer day. I may have put on a harness to keep me secure to a parachute, but it felt like I had donned a superhero outfit that set me free. Someone had ripped the door of my prison open and gave me a taste of the outside world. I felt like I could do anything. For the first time in my life, I felt a sense of confidence.

This newfound feeling was interesting. I wasn't sure how to deal with it, and there was still that lingering fear of things that could go wrong. It didn't make any problems go away. I still had very few friends, as well as being somewhat socially inept. Being gay didn't help things much. But I had a taste of something I never had before, and it was more addicting than the comfort that solitude had given me. I felt alive. I realized I had wasted too much time hiding and playing it safe. I needed to allow myself to explore myself and the world and start living.

Armed with this confidence, I set myself the challenge of dealing with my introversion and embracing my sexuality while not hiding it from others. Both were challenges that scared me, but I was determined to no longer ignore them. It didn't start well. One day I took the bus to a pub with the intent to socialize and made it to the door of the pub before turning around and going home. But it was a start.

I decided a better way to start this adventure would be at curling which was soon to begin. It was already a comfortable environment for me. As if the world read my mind, a team from the local LGBT league happened to join my Wednesday Men's League for the 2017/18 season. Matthew was their third and was perhaps one of the most extroverted people I had ever met. It seemed he could strike up a conversation with anybody - a complete opposite of me. Of course, Matthew would be the guy I would have a huge crush on.

I would normally have ignored my feelings. I had crushes on guys before. But this time, after a couple months, I mustered up the courage to ask Matthew out. I jumped from a plane. This should be easy. To my surprise, Matthew said yes, and we ended up dating for the rest of the season. During this time, he brought me into his circle of friends in the LGBTQ+ community. As I slowly opened myself to them, I felt more and more confident about myself. This pretty much outed me at the curling club.

I made many changes to my life when I was dating Matthew and into the following summer of 2018 after we ended things. I left my position at the university and went into the private sector to further my career. I began to make a conscious effort to overcome my introversion and insert myself into social situations more often. When an opportunity came up to join Matthew's curling team in the LGBT League, I took it – Matthew was leaving town to further his career. I told my mom I was gay.

With the summer ending, and the 2018 curling season about to start, I went full throttle into my adventure. I jumped right into the LGBT League, determined to make my new team proud and make some new friends. That entire season was a year of self-exploration as I found so many more reasons to be confident and proud of myself. While I made some stupid decisions, I made some good ones too.

For the first time, I took chances and allowed others to see my failures and successes. I met new people, forged close friendships, and discovered new pastimes. That skydive two years ago had taught me that nothing truly good was going to happen if I didn't take a chance. I learned that staying safe was no way to live. That experience ripped me out of that prison I was hiding in at 200 kilometers an hour, and I've never turned back.

Alphabet of Hope

Laying in this hammock, waiting to skydive again, I am taken aback at how much I have grown in the last couple of years. I thought I knew who I was, but in reality, I had no clue at all. I didn't know what it was like to truly live, and now I finally feel like I am, and I don't want to stop.

"We're up! Get your gear on!"

My friend Steve is shouting at me, letting me know we are next. Finally! It's a big day for both of us. I get to thank the man who pushed me out of that same plane and opened my eyes. It's my 100th skydive today, a milestone for every skydiver. I am giving Steve the honour of joining me. He is as stoked about it as I am. Time to put my parachute on and jump off a perfectly good plane!

Not where I thought I'd be two years ago. Go figure.

Alphabet of Hope

Coming Into Myself

Written By Alex Masse

I remember being young and hating everything feminine. Most people wouldn't believe that looking at me now in my pink dresses, hair alive with bows and ribbons. It's true, though: I was your typical tomboy.

I disliked traditionally feminine clothes for a number of reasons: sensory issues, laziness, and most of all, not wanting boys to give me attention. I'd put on dresses for a nice dinner or fancy gathering, but it wasn't something I went out of my way to do, because it wasn't a way I wanted to be seen. In my younger self's eyes, dolling up meant being looked at by boys in a very particular way.

To say everything changed when I realized I liked women would be an understatement. Suddenly, I wanted to care about my looks, because they didn't exist in a patriarchal prison: it didn't matter how men perceived me. I could look pretty for myself, and to catch the eyes of women who loved other women. I was drawn to lesbian history, and butch/femme culture. I identified with almost everything I read about femmes, and followed in their footsteps. It was an equation that finally had a solution when men were removed. Being able to pick and choose feminine aspects and performing them for myself and other women made the whole thing inherently freeing and less frightening.

My struggles with identity didn't end there. I realized that my relationship to some aspects of typical womanhood, like makeup or chest growth, didn't appeal to me at all. I knew what I was, and I knew what I wanted, but there was the undeniable sense that something else was going on. It wasn't just that I didn't *care* for some aspects of femininity. There was more to it than indifference.

I didn't realize that was the case until I was venting to a friend about it: I talked about how makeup made me feel like my face in the mirror belonged to someone else, how it distorted my reflection, and my friend said rather plainly that I was dealing with "textbook dysphoria." There were other triggers, too: sometimes I wished I had a flat chest, sometimes I'd shave and regret it for days after. I always thought I was subversive woman at best, and a "fake femme lesbian" on bad days. After all, what kind of femme freaks out when she puts on makeup?

Except being femme was never about having the reddest lipstick or the best fake lashes. Being femme for me meant a femininity that you can play with and fully own, and something that is inherently lesbian in its expression and interpretation. It's about that privilege to pick and choose what aspects of femininity you perform, and what you don't.

I remember reading about those who knew they were lesbians, but not necessarily women. That you could be the former without being the latter, that lesbian was a gender in itself. Most nonbinary lesbians I heard about were butch, but if a butch can feel that way, why not a femme? I might be feminine, but that doesn't make me a woman. I often wear femininity the way a drag queen does: it's fun, but it's my plaything. I'll twist it and push it and extend it to its limits, to being unrecognizable.

There was also an undeniable euphoria in being outright androgynous. I loved my eccentric ways of performing femininity, but I also *adored* being androgynous. I wore suits, used they/them pronouns, the works. People would see my face and ask if I was a boy or a girl. Sometimes they'd call me "it." At least some of them were trying to hurt my feelings, but they had *no* idea, the euphoria and validation that washed over me. Their confusion was my victory.

Despite all these signs, literally everyone knew I was nonbinary before I was. People confided in how they loved looking up to me as a nonbinary role model, mentioned it offhandedly, and when I did eventually come out, some friends actually said, "Weren't you out already?"

The "a-ha" moment came when a friend and artistic collaborator tagged me in a nonbinary meme. I don't know why, but that's when it clicked. I don't even remember the post, it was something about having nonbinary friends?

But gosh, that changed everything. I'd been questioning it for some time, deep down, but being seen as nonbinary by a friend made it all click into place. Like all of a sudden, it didn't matter that I was feminine, or femme, or a lesbian. I was still nonbinary.

It can be strange to reconcile, being nonbinary and a lesbian. A lot of people don't understand it: "Doesn't lesbian mean a woman attracted to women?"

And yes, in theory, it does. But like I said, lots of lesbians have felt a separation from womanhood, to some degree or another. After all, so much of a woman's role in cisheteropatriarchal society is being with a man.

I remember the stories I've heard. The nonbinary lesbians I've known. I don't see why this identity can't coexist with my being a femme.

For the record, by the way, nonbinary encompasses anyone that isn't 100% a man or woman. I still have some attachment to womanhood, and absolutely no attachment to being a man, so there's no reason why there's anything less than lesbian about a woman being attracted to me.

Sure, we aren't the most visible. I don't look like how some people think femmes should, with long hair and makeup and the ability to joke about "looking straight." I don't look like how some people think nonbinary people should, binding and contouring in a strive to perfect androgyny.

When it comes to my gender, I keep to the closet. Not because I'm ashamed or afraid, but because it's an exhausting conversation, and I know some folks might never understand. I bite back a sigh when people call me "ma'am." I grudgingly check the "F" box when papers ask for my gender, simply to avoid being questioned. I don't owe people my complexities.

Hell, even if I tried for that perfect androgyny? I'd still get misgendered. There's no way to "look" nonbinary, after all.

There were times that I stood up for my identity that didn't work out; I had a friend who made a group chat exclusively for cis women. When she found out that I was nonbinary, she bombarded me with questions about that identity and how it fit into the context of that group chat.

I thought she was open to being educated, so I explained my identity, and went on to say that I didn't belong in her group of women, but that trans women did.

The mask fell off: she called me biologically female, said she was speaking scientifically, and the whole shebang.

It's a privilege, for your biggest battle to be getting people to see you, for who you really are. I know that there are people in the trans community who risk being attacked, beaten, or worse. I know people who *wish* they blended in, wish they didn't get the odd looks for fear for their lives in public.

I owe a lot to my trans siblings. Without saying a word, they tell the world so much.

One day, I'll have that bravery.

It's definitely a mouthful, nonbinary femme lesbian. The words are a package deal: femme links to lesbian, lesbian to nonbinary, so on and so on, a web of integral pieces to my identity gloriously interwoven.

It just feels right. I'm so happy that I've figured myself out, and so happy that I'm me. As I grow braver, I'll get bolder. In the meantime, surrounding myself with people who understand and respect my identity is invaluable.

When I was figuring myself out, I wrote one of my first poems about gender identity. The last stanza went something like this:

I am a message on a billboard that got painted over.

I'm an unofficial constellation, a connection unorthodox.

I'm badly-traced, I'm cobbled-together, I'm cheaply-made, I'm out of tune,

I'm a soup gone too sweet.

Fine by me.

I was never meant to be eaten anyway.

It's still true today: I am not to be eaten. Not by men, not by the binary, not by any person or any system.

And I couldn't be more lucky.

Demi Means Half

Written By McRae

Half a person. Half a sexuality. Lost in the grey-spectrum like a piece of chalk in a snowstorm. Demisexuality is this weird, strange, niche place that's home to exactly the sort of people one would expect - brilliant, beautiful, and enigmatic creatures obsessed with essence over form. People who often attempt to see beyond form, rooting around in a person's ribcage to rip out their soul and see it for what it truly is.

Perhaps it's easier to just fade into the background of heteronormativity, when it comes to being Demi. For all intents and purposes, you blend into the crowd. While there's this sort of common reality to be shared with bisexual folks, it's always a strange question - what are the conditions that would make you date or love against your previously established cisgendered presentation to the world? How deeply do you want Judith Butler to peer into your windows, shaking her fist at your cowardice, yelling at you to be who you were born to be?

I'm not the first thing you expect to see when anyone first hears the word "demisexual." Hell, I didn't even know the word existed until I was already twenty-two or twenty-three years old. Growing up in a very machismo-based home, the son of two generations of loggers and lumberjacks, I was only aware of a fraction of the sexuality spectrum! There were heteronormative people (not that I knew that word or what the fuck it meant!) And that was it!

Until I met one of my mentors in high school, one of only a few "out" people in my tiny town… Well, I barely understood what being gay was! I was one hundred percent the dudebro disabled kid that walked and talked tough to protect my fragile ego. Getting into scraps to defend some false honor - what my idea of a "man" was at the time. It's not a unique story. It's common to so many small towns across North America. It's a sad story, with sad themes - repression, hurt, fear, and hatred.

By the time I hit university, I knew that I was definitely not the macho logger that I had been expected to grow into. I waffled, thinking back to my dope queer drama-teacher lesbian role model, and flapped about - wondering if I was gay myself. Was that why I felt so different and never seemed to fit in? While the story of my disability is often wrapped up in the story of my sexuality, these were genuine philosophical debates I would have with myself.

"Why do I feel a deep connection and attraction to some people, but not others?"

"Am I just being an artsy-fartsy weirdo? Why don't I just drop it?"

"I hate myself because I don't understand myself."

I wish that last one was unique to just me, but I know that self-loathing and uncertainty is a thread that everybody in the LGBTQ+ spectrum often encounters. By the time I got to the last few years of my undergraduate degree, I was exiting a toxic relationship based heavily in heteronormative relationship paths. If I had been confused before, I was even more confused when all my friends came out of the woodwork letting me know how grateful they were that I was free of that person!

I finally learned about demisexuality through the one place most queer folk wander through - the internet, of course! What? I don't understand! I always thought "ace" was something rappers from the UK used to mean "good!"

See, demisexuality works slightly differently for everyone, but at the root, your attraction and lust is related to your emotional bond with a person. You simply can't force it! (Unless you want some veeeeery awkward conversations as a person with certain types of organs concerning the possibility of erectile dysfunction!)

Ah…

It can mean you're not into people sexually? It can mean you're less into people sexually?! There's a romantic side to being within the grey spectrum!?

Talk about revelations.

But unfortunately, it was as confusing as it was enlightening. In that era of late-aughts tumblr-subcultures, I was forced to sift through community after community as I slowly grew as a person.

I learned that one could be asexual OR aromantic, meaning they could want romance or sex or both or neither and still be considered ace! How queer!

Pun intended.

I had loved my previous partners, and of course I had enjoyed sex with them. But I always failed to really be that horn-dog male stereotype. Comments on bodies and quotients of "sexiness" would zoom by about eight feet above my head! I'd always want to have these deep philosophical and intellectual conversations with people I went on dates with. Hell, the age of Tinder was a godsend, as it allowed me to sift through all the people that didn't really want to get to know the "real me" MUCH easier!

Regardless, I've considered as to whether I might be sapiosexual or not, which is an attraction to intelligence as far as I understand it, but I found myself loving and being with people who weren't necessarily PhD candidates or rocket scientists over the years. It definitely added to the confusion!

By the time I started to figure it out at twenty-four or so, I had noticed a few things. The first was that my partner usually came first in regard to our "dalliances," one could say. Pun partially intended. The second was that I needed to spend lots of time with people before I could even potentially become sexually attracted to them. And many people I never saw as more than a friend or acquaintance no matter what happened! There was this sort of "bonding period" that I always encountered with each new partner I would end up dating. I also continued to lean more towards female-presenting people as a matter of comfort, but there were a very small handful of male-presenting people that I could see myself dating and being with sexually. I must confess I definitely leaned into being a bit of a cock-tease regardless…

It's nice to feel wanted, right?

While I'm much more responsible now, I feel like I've finally settled into my sexuality. If it gives any hope for folks younger than I, it wasn't until my late twenties that it started to happen! When I date now, it's kind of nice to approach each new relationship without a sexual subtext, as much as it may at times frustrate those whom I go on dates with! Not that I can't appreciate the plethora of bear-bodied lumberjack fantasies that exist of course, even if I'm not really much for jumping right into those fantasies!

Growth comes at different rates for different people, and the journey of self-discovery is often one of the hardest to travel. Some folks aren't sure of their gender or sexuality until very late in life, and I'm at least glad that I could figure it out before I made anyone too unhappy by jumping into marriage or the act of having children without being able to express my demisexuality in a way that felt right.

While sometimes I still revel in the caricature of the big, white, bearded lumberjack wearing flannel… It IS nice to feel wanted as I mentioned before… It's also nice knowing that I'm doing so as an expression of my identity as it relates to my history and upbringing rather than simply as someone's sexual fantasy. I mostly date women now, simply because of that whole heteronormativity thing, but it's nice knowing that the right spark could change everything!

If you don't have it figured out, but feel pressured to do so, why not take a moment and reflect on why you might be racing to figure out who you are in the first place?!

I mean…

What's the rush?

Why not do what feels right in the moment? The kindhearted and accepting people around you shouldn't care if you change your mind later, or if you realize something new about yourself that adds context and belonging to who you are! Learning is lifelong, right?

Figuring out who you are just isn't something that can be rushed.

Good luck out there! And remember, "demi" means half. And you don't want to be half a person!

Or do you?...

Enjoy Your Ride on the Emotional Rollercoaster of Love

Written By David J.C. Smith

When I met him, we had the most romantic summer of love. We were both living in different states but spent the summer working on the same roller coaster at an amusement park. We worked together and immediately had a strong connection that evolved from friends into a full-on romance. The kicker was, he was still in the closet, coming from the bible belt, and his high school sweetheart/ longtime girlfriend was also working at the park. He hadn't fully realized or accepted that he was gay. He was "bi-curious" and became one of those where I, the fully open and confident gay guy, had helped him experience affection and intimacy for another man; all behind his girlfriend's back. He was "waiting for marriage" with his girlfriend so he was also a bona fide virgin in regard to sexual contact.

While we both knew it was just for the summer, I had fallen hard for him. We had shared our most intimate secrets, even things he has never shared with his girlfriend or anybody else. My young heart was hoping that one day, he and I would be together. After the summer was over when we went back home, we texted and sexted almost every day. He went through periods of guilt and such that any closeted gay guy from a conservative religious background goes through and tried to just be friends, which I respected. However, it still always came back to us talking to each other as lovers, most often at his behest.

A year later, he came to visit me, and we spent a week together catching up on a lot of things and spent the week essentially making love. He went back home, and we continued our long distance "friendship" until a year or two later. He seemed to start to lose interest as he went back to work at the amusement park and met new friends, including one that he said he fell in love with but who was legitimately straight. Slowly our "friendship" withered away until I, feeling depressed about the whole thing, sent him a scathing email that evolved into a huge fight and changed everything between us. We lost touch for a couple years. I regret what I said in that email today, but then I was driven solely on a broken heart and frustration that he wanted to maintain his relationship with his girlfriend when it was so clear that it wouldn't last.

A few years later, he gets back in touch and announces that he is marrying his girlfriend, the same one he had back in our time at the park and invites me to the wedding. It brought back a rush of old feelings of love, but I kept them to myself and went to attend his wedding, I brought my boyfriend to the wedding, and we were the only male-male couple in attendance. It was in a small town in the bible belt- intimidating and a bit scary, but fortunately we didn't have a problem. What the married couple didn't know is that I am a wicked line dancer. So at the reception when all of the 'white people wedding songs' came on, I made their jaws drop by showing off that at least one person there could dance. Since it was his wedding day and he was focused on the event, we didn't get to spend much time chatting or catching up, which I was okay with. It was his day; I was happy for him and I wanted him to enjoy it.

After the wedding, we stayed in touch and he told me that, for his honeymoon, they are planning a road trip through my state. He asked if they could come visit and stay the night at my place 1 or 2 nights to save money. Of course, it's okay. I also give them some suggestions of cool landmarks they can visit during their trip. The first night they were in town, they got a hotel room, but him, his wife, my boyfriend (the same one from the wedding) and I met up for dinner at a local restaurant. His wife and my boyfriend were bored as hell as he and I caught up, like old friends who never lost touch we just talked for hours and hours. However, the sexual tension between the two of us needed quite a sharp knife to cut. The next day, when they did spend the night. He and his wife were sleeping in their own bed, and I was in mine. He told me later on that he was tempted to sneak out of his bed and join me in mine for an hour or two. I wish he had, but wisely, he did not.

When they left, I bid them goodbye, and we fell out of touch again. Three years later, he got back in touch with the same ole "why haven't we talked in so long" to which I responded that he never responded to any of my messages, so I figured he didn't want to be friends and I wanted to move on. To which he finally drops the bomb…

"So, I am going to come out as gay, and divorce my wife."

I mean, shocker, right? but he needed a friend for advice and moral support, so I was happy to provide. Especially since I was only a very small number of people he could confide in. I thought, "Wow, now is the time I can finally tell him that I have been in love with him for all these years and be with him." But before I could, he tells me the story of how he met a guy last year and they've been secretly "dating" behind his wife's back. I ended up with a broken heart yet again and didn't tell him how I felt. But I was there for him through all the emotions and fear he was going through as he prepared to embark on his coming out and the uncertainty of coming out as gay while married to a woman in the bible belt.

My first question was "did you have any kids?" Thankfully, no. Second question, I asked him how his first sexual experience with his wife (and first woman) went, especially since they had been waiting for marriage. He explained that he struggled with getting aroused and was able to brush it off as exhaustion while exploring other sexual acts that did not necessarily involve penetration. As a conservative couple in a Bible belt small town, being sexually adventurous wasn’t exactly on the menu.

After that summer, we didn't talk much until a few months later when he packed his whole life, left the bible belt, and moved to Chicago. He had broken up with this "boyfriend" and yet again, I was there for emotional support. I was ready to drop my "L" bomb when before I could, he told me he had met someone there he was now living with. Again, broken hearted, but it was clear we still both harbored feelings for each other and occasional exchanged hot pictures and sexted. I was holding out hope that maybe I would finally get what I had been longing for. This emotional experience for me, at this point, had killed at least two different relationships (over different time periods) with guys I was dating because it stopped me from developing feelings for them. I feel bad now, because I was a completely jerk to them and no doubt left them with a broken heart. An experience they did not deserve and that I hope they have since found happiness in their lives.

Finally, I just said, “fuck it” and in my own emotional puke, I told him I was in love with him and wanted to be with him. I just let it all out there. He essentially responded with, "I love you too," but in the same sentence, put me right into the friendzone. We stayed "friends" with him on Facebook but distanced myself a bit from him and unfollowed him when the posts with him and his Chicago boyfriend became too emotional for me in the vein hope of moving on.

About 6 months later, I still hadn't gotten over him and every few months we chatted. It always made my heart would flutter. So, I told him I wanted to come visit him for a few days in Chicago. It was during the travel off season, so I booked a cheap flight and a nice hotel room for cheap in the Boystown area of Chicago. I was looking forward to a few days of us catching up on some intimacy, adventures, and just spending time together. What he didn't know was that after years of toiling in emotional turmoil over him, this trip was going to be the decisive moment that I would decide whether to continue to pursue him or move on with my life. At this point, it had been ten years since we first met, I was at the end of my 20s and contemplating other life changing things as well.

During my visit, we had some sexy and non-sexy fun times. However, I had realized that while it had been 10 years since we met, his emotional self was invested elsewhere and while he was beginning to explore his gay self, we were two different people. I had left Chicago with the answer I was seeking when I arrived. I got on the plane, with a sense of closure and happiness that at this point we were in different directions in our life. A relationship was simply not going to happen. I felt like a huge emotional burden was lifted off my shoulders and was ready to pursue new things in my life. It was truly freeing.

Alphabet of Hope

Finding the Beauty Queen in Me

Written By Parker Chapple

I cannot find the beauty queen that I am looking for. She has my name, or more accurately, I have hers. A contestant in the Miss Canada pageant somewhere between 1970–1975.

When asked, mother enthusiastically quips "Oh yes, as soon as we heard it, your father and I looked at each other and just knew, someday we would name our daughter that, is that not strange? How we just knew?"

Its rather bothersome that they knew who I was to be, and yet to me it's still somewhat allusive.

My father was a navy man. He was a firefighter for 30 years, retiring as captain only a few years ago. He is a charming strong-man type, that other men either want to fight or aspire to be, while his keen moral compass alludes to his deep compassion just enough for women to swoon and get giggly at.

My mother is all things excessively feminine, something that inspired my gifting her a "bedazzler", knowing it would be put to good use. She is fiercely loyal, dependably stalwart and so fearlessly honest, I've learned to not ask her opinion unless I'm emotionally prepared for the consequences of her conviction.

My parents were divorced by the time I was born, therefore being primarily raised by my other, a descendant of Anglo-Saxon heritage, I was instructed on the requirements of being a lady. A "Ms." who only speaks when spoken too, a "Miss" who is intelligently well mannered, and proper "Lady" who could exceed the expectations her namesake bestowed.

I am not a Ms, Miss or Lady; and I don't wear dresses.

I am taller than most of my female bodied counterparts, with broad shoulders, small chest, narrow hips and a squashy midsection that forecasts my emotional state better than I am often able to interpret it. I'm an outspoken, dynamic adventure seeker who bores easily and will almost always fight for the underdog. I have tattoos, body piercings, black boots, collared button ups, and cheeky T-shirts that imply my political and social leanings. You can hear my laugh long before you can see me in the crowd, but should you get lost, I'm the one bubbling with enthusiasm somewhere in the middle, and I am neither boy nor girl.

It's true that I am equipped with the body parts that should easily designate me to one or the other. But, as many of us queers have learned, gender is defined by two things; the society I engage with, and how I feel about it.

I am most aware of my gender disparity on special occasions, when a person is supposed to get "dressed up". Do I wear a tie? Do I straighten my hair into a sleek pompadour, or flaunt my messy curls? Do I wear make up to only even out my skin tone, or do I pull out the eyeshadow palette and mascara? should I bind my breasts so that my suspenders lay flat brandishing my angular shoulders, or wear a bra and leave my collar open enough to spark confused interest? Through the course of the evening. I will likely pull out the lip-gloss, straighten my tie, fluff my hair to astounding heights, and wonder if I should have dabbed sparkles to the corner of my eyelids so that I could flutter them enticingly while attempting to flirt.

Generally, I've learned to revel in the shadow of my freak flag. However, there are still times where I am desperate to reconcile the anxiety of aligning myself to how world thinks I should be, and who I am. There are many more when I don't know where the definition of one ends, and I begin. And there are those times when all I want is my damned coffee, and don't have the energy to explain I am not a ma'am, because well, I have not yet had my damned coffee.

I have often wondered if I am who I am because I was raised with a keen sense of what a man or woman should be. Perhaps after so many failed attempts of not fitting into either, I picked up the prettiest and most handsome of their broken pieces to keep for myself.

What is certain, is that I will continue to do my best loving all of it. No matter my assumed body shape, perceived intellectual qualification, alleged emotional brevity or distinct wardrobe selection on hand. I will continue learning to love me, just as I am:

A sometimes beauty queen, warrior king, wayward peasant, ardent friend and lover of chocolate cake with vanilla icing.

Growing Into a Queer Identity

Written By Brett Grunerud

My dad always told me that the single most dangerous thing that an average person does in their life will be driving a car; and I believe him. But no driving conditions, weather events, or perilous roadways ever made me as nervous as the night driving up the freeway with my best friend shortly after New Year's 2018. I was rehearsing what and how to say my planned coming out to her. We had been best friends since third grade and, of course, she and I remain best friends to this day. It had been a rough fall and winter that year, my first year of university fresh out of high school. I had been playing a game unknown to my friends and family; seeing someone that I liked more and more while finally allowing myself to admit that I liked guys. No one really knew except for me, and I loved this fact. I was able to accept who I was and enjoy it without having to do what I really did not want to do – admit this to those around me.

Growing up, the whole concept of people with sexualities other than straight was really not something that was on my radar. I had no experience with meeting or being around anyone who was gay, bisexual, trans, gender non-conforming, or any other part of the LGBTQI+ community; at least not out, or something which was talked about. Growing up in a smaller city in Saskatchewan, my family, both close and extended, ranged from somewhat to very conservative in both politics and mindset. There was never any outward hate speech or direct conversation about homosexuality, but from jokes that everyone chuckled at in family gatherings to comments made here or there, I thought that it was not something you wanted to be, not something that you wanted others thinking about you or viewing you, something that one should avoid in conversation and in relation. I recall especially the thought passed around that you should avoid being *perceived* as gay by others; no limp wrists or feminine traits should be shown, especially in public.

Moving away from Saskatchewan to British Columbia when I was seven was a big move for my family. The rest of my elementary and high schooling was done in my new hometown and I made friendships that I still have today. Since my very young years in Northern Saskatchewan, a lot of growing occurred in my immediate family. Although 'gayness' was still a concept never spoken about, I also hadn't heard anything negative on the concept and it was largely forgotten to me as something to be cognisant of. That all changed in my first year of high school, eighth grade where I lived. Entering high school, my small group of friends expanded into something somewhat larger. One day, out of the blue, my good friend approached me and simply asked

"Brett, would you be friends with someone who is gay?" Not wanting to answer incorrectly or be perceived 'wrong', of course I simply answered

"No, I don't think so." Nothing seemed out of place after I answered but suddenly, I did not hear from this friend. I knew he was still spending time with everyone in the group but conveniently not if I was present. I really had no idea what was going on, until finally, one morning, I got on the daily bus to school and went to sit beside my best friend. Finally, I asked her what on earth was up with our mutual friend.

She looked at me almost as if I was dumb, and said, “Brett, he came out last month. He’s gay and you said you didn’t want gay friends.”

I don’t really remember my reply to her; knowing my meek high school self I probably tried to deny or deflect my fault. But I do remember the feeling the second she said those words to me. It was like someone had shocked me, I felt hollow and red hot with embarrassment and shame. Suddenly the concept of being gay was not just a concept about a group of people that I would never encounter and I saw all at once what being gay actually meant: nothing. It was simply liking someone else, just like any other of the fun and many crushes that passed around the school. All it meant was that someone loved different people. My thoughts raced; I knew that I missed seeing my friend, I knew that so many, especially at school, would actively *choose* to bully and be horrible about being different in any way. I realised the vulnerability and incredible strength of my friend, all required simply to be himself. I realised that more than just abandoning my friend in a time which he should have support, joy, relief, and reassurance, I actively had been one of those people who put him down and participated in the uphill battle and what must had been turmoil inside that he had to face. I still look back on this day often; it has been the most influential day on my maturity, education, and actual perception of the entire world around me.

Thankfully, after an apology, my friend allowed me to be part of his life. Over the next few years in high school, the friend group grew and included different sexualities and gender identities. My family's social views grew too, all of my friends were welcomed without question to any and all events, though there was a learning curve. I began to volunteer more and, still relatively closed-minded compared to today, sought out opportunities to get involved in the community through volunteering with various organizations which continued to teach me about the world.

Looking back, it was about the tenth grade where I noticed a 'problem'. I was looking at guys and was liking what I saw. Of course, no worries, as I had a solution and explanation. It was simply a phase! My online research showed that many guys seemed to have a phase like this, reassuring. I firmly believed that one day, the perfect girl, my soulmate, would find me and it would snap me out of it and that would be the end of any kind of phase. Armed with these thoughts, I never allowed myself to even think about the subject; it wasn't something I needed to be concerned about because after all, it was just a waiting game. I was involved with as many activities and volunteer groups as I could; by eleventh and twelfth grade I had meetings most lunch hours and was off after school doing something probably six days of the week. I kept my friend group, gained new friends, and obviously in hindsight was in deep, deep denial. My mind was busy, I was home to eat and sleep, and I gave myself no opportunity to consider the matter of my sexuality in any form. I avoided any conversations about crushes or sex, I had ready-to-go responses ready in case there was an unavoidable conversation or truth-or-dare game.

It was the early twilight hours one morning in June or July, just after finishing high school. Everyone at the house was still passed out from many, many shots the night before. I was wide awake. I felt like I had just been slammed by a ton of bricks because I realized, or allowed myself to realize for the first time, that I was gay. I did not have anything against gay people; I didn't feel ashamed and had always loved seeing my proud friends and educating others about the matter. The sudden thought of having to come out was nauseating. I thought that I had worked so hard to achieve what I had: good grades, various friend groups, involvement in the community, and of course my personality. I was getting ready to attend university that Fall in my city with most of my friends. I pondered what would happen if I came out, sitting there in the post-party mess. I saw the thoughts of those who I would tell; of course, I'd have support from all of my friends and family too, but I was worried.

The separation of pre-gay and post-gay Brett would be suddenly made to the world. All of the aspects of my life: my interests, personality, accomplishments and everything else would be associated with me being gay, and that scared me. I wouldn't be funny because I was Brett, I would be funny because I was gay; I wouldn't be smart or hardworking because that is who I am, but because I was gay. I was very worried that people would think my love of the community and volunteering in it would all be related to my sexuality. Everything from what I wore to specific actions I took would be due to me being gay and suddenly, if I came out, I would become gay-Brett. Of course, with more hindsight added, these were rather ridiculous fears, but these were the very things that consumed my thoughts day in and out after that morning. I wouldn't watch TV with my family, just in case I looked a little too long at an actor or gay scene. I looked down everywhere I walked, just in case someone saw me looking at a cute passerby and made the association.

I spent that summer between high school and university exploring. Once in university, I was seeing a boy I really liked most evenings, all in complete secrecy. I would leave my friends in the library at eight o'clock and get home at eleven; I'm sure my family was amazed at my studious nature. I was not sleeping, I was not eating well or much, but I thought that I was handling it well and doing a good job keeping it all a secret. Towards the end of the first semester, I realised that somebody had a bigger mouth than I thought and my whole game was becoming an open secret, but unconfirmed, among my circle of friends. My best friend came to see me for the first time in a few months at this time during final exams. She was shocked and asked if I was alright; I was dumbfounded by what she meant but, again looking back, it was obvious. I had lost weight, and generally looked badly run down. I laughed it off and we began our Winter break.

Once on break, again I worked out a solution. I really saw that coming out was going to happen, either by me or by word of mouth from others. I also realised how exhausted I was after my first semester at university; I had come out of it with grades that I liked and all aspects of my life how I wanted them, but I really began to doubt that I could do it over again for another semester, let alone the rest of school or life. I decided while sitting in my basement on New Year's that I would not let another year go by keeping my secret. After all, I had come to terms with people knowing, was happy with who I was, and finally figured out that I did not need to value anyone who would react badly to who I was. Within a few days, all of my close friends were told. The most surprising thing, to me, was how surprised everyone was when I told them,

I had after all been extremely excited about the upcoming ‘Love, Simon’ release. I was warmly accepted and with this confidence I turned my attention to my last ‘hurdle’: coming out to my family.

For the next five months I attempted to tell my parents. Every night I would work myself up, while watching TV all together after dinner, to just blurt it out. Each and every time I would lose my nerve and simply say goodnight and go downstairs. I tried again and again; my parents even commented on how ‘antsy’ I had become. Finally, summer came around and I was working full time at a campground. Towards the end of May, my birthday was approaching. The night before my birthday, I quickly typed up a note to my family. On my way out of the door for my shift the next day, I left the letter and left with my phone turned off. Being someone who has to overanalyse anything, and the months of leadup to finally leaving my note, I had a friend ready to go and get clothes if needed from my house. I really did not think that I had anything to worry about with coming out to my family; they had learned a lot and welcomed all of my friends without question, but when it is your child coming out I worried things could be different. I was right not to worry about my family’s reaction, it was a peaceful acknowledgment in all aspects and, I felt like I was finally done.

In the few years since coming out, I feel like I have come into my own and been able to appreciate myself for who I am. My fears about how those would see me melted away and I was able to be myself, without having to overthink every action. It really felt like a weight was lifted from my chest and like I could breathe freely. I quickly learned to not pay attention to what others thought of me; within the first few months of being out I was called both too gay and not gay enough. Being gay is a part of who I am and has afforded me a large 'chosen family' in addition to my family. I am so proud of the LGBTQI+ community and proud to be a part of it; but am anxious about many growing problems within it such as racism, gatekeeping, and the poor treatment of trans and non-conforming people within it. There is still a lot left for my family and I to work through and learn, something that even the most accepting family must do from time-to-time. I look forward to my future, and hope whoever reading this may also.

Hope and Guidance from the Future

Written By Micah Porter

Dear Micah,

I hope this letter finds you happy and well. I would suggest you try and read this when you are in a good place emotionally, with a mindset that allows you to be both reflective and forward thinking. Knowing you better than you know yourself, you will benefit from these suggestions.

As you read this, you are just shy of your 18th birthday on January 4, 1991. As I write this, it is 2020, and I will be 48 on that same day. I am hoping the 30 years between us can provide some loving and important guidance for you.

I choose to share this with you for a number of reasons. First, you are officially entering adulthood. You will mature tremendously over the next several years, in all ways, but your upcoming birthday does mark a milestone. I don't want you to react impulsively, worry too much, or struggle understanding everything that is in this letter. But today, December 21, will be a critical day for you in the future, a day of celebration for both your mental and physical health. Caring for these aspects of your whole self will be some of the most significant keys to your future health and happiness.

Let's start with where you are right now. Your college years will be some of the best of your life. In high school, your work and commitment in the classroom and athletic arena has afforded you the opportunity to be a scholarship student-athlete at Hillsdale College. Celebrate that achievement. Soak up the experiences of traveling the country and competing as a track & field athlete. Hold dear the relationships developed with your teammates, coaches, professors, and others on campus. They will be important and long lasting.

Your 20s will be a whirlwind of change. After college, you will pack up your Ford Ranger and find yourself amidst the mountains of Colorado to start your career as an educator and coach. Excitement and fear will overwhelm you in this journey. Embrace both. You will soon get married to a woman, buy a house, adopt your daughter, and have a son, all before your 26th birthday. Fatherhood will be very exciting for you, and you will pour your heart and soul into your family.

You will also begin drinking … heavily. Alcohol will become a poison in your life, and you will use it to bury a whole host of emotions and feelings that you have been harboring for years. Unfortunately, you will turn to alcohol during this time to numb yourself from addressing these deeper feelings. Your genetic make-up will put you in a very vulnerable state with this drug. Do not ignore the dangerous grip it will have on you. Physically, your young body will be able to handle the excess you subject it to, but inevitably, alcohol will slowly and steadily begin to devour your body, self, and soul.

Despite becoming an alcoholic, you will enter your 30s as a successful educator and accomplished coach. Your hard work and commitment to your craft will bring you much admiration and accolades. Be humbled by them. Your drinking will also reach a dangerous level in your early 30s, and signs of physical and mental decay will become increasingly apparent to yourself and those around you. Your family, and especially your children, will suffer as collateral damage from your addiction. The lasting impact it will have on each of your relationships will leave many scars.

It will also be in these years that you begin to truly acknowledge that you are a gay man. You always knew it, but have avoided this reality, ignored your feelings, and numbed yourself with alcohol and the storybook heteronormative life that you thought you were supposed to pursue. You will enroll in conversion therapy. Your doctor will prescribe medication for depression. You will have your first liver biopsy and you will be diagnosed with liver steatosis, a pre-cirrhosis disease caused from your drinking. Your mental and physical health will begin to deteriorate dangerously fast, and it will become increasingly clear that something drastic needs to change. You will know what you need to do.

At 37, you will tell your wife and two children that you are gay. Your reality will begin to collapse all around you while simultaneously revealing a whole new Universe with glimpses of happiness, health, and truth. This new Universe will bring you to the love of your life, Brandan. Though several years your younger, his wisdom, intellect, and honesty will provide a guiding light through very difficult times.

You will make many, many mistakes in your relationships with your children during these years. Time will help to heal some wounds, but others will feel very permanent. Keep trying to repair them and be patient and respectful of what they need to work through the pain that they endured. Even as I write this, I have much hope that things will get better.

The love that will develop between you and Brandan will be one that you never thought possible. We will be celebrating our 10th Anniversary together this spring 2021. There is much to share with you about the beauty of this man and the love and partnership that he will bring to your life, but I am going to let you enjoy that paradise on your own. What I will share with you is that Brandan will be by your side, even as your alcoholism carries into your new life. And on December 21, 2016, on a cold, rainy winter night, after your addiction and choices nearly destroy the most loving and important relationship in your life, Brandan will drive you to your first AA meeting.

From here, there is no looking back. Your 40s will be your best years thus far. You will evolve from surviving to thriving. You will work to truly understand the mental health challenges you struggled with in your early years. Shame be gone, your mental clarity and awareness will be resurrected. You will rediscover your love of exercise. Your body will heal, grow, and look better than it ever has. The lifestyle and home you and Brandan will build together, will birth a level of emotional, physical, and mental happiness that you have never experienced.

Your career will also take-off during this time. With Brandan's encouragement and support, you will challenge yourself with new opportunities and become a successful and influential school leader. Your love of education will only grow in these years. Your continued commitment to LGBTQ+ advocacy for youth and athletics will rapidly advance, and you will find great joy in this work.

There is so much yet to come in your young life. And I love you very, very much. It took me a long time to say that to myself.

Just like in sports, which you know very well, you need to be broken down before you can grow to new heights. Don't get discouraged. Keep nourishing the things you hold dear: kindness, love, hard work, along with your scrawny grit. They will all help you lift yourself out of your depths. And never reject the hand of others as they reach into to help you. Their strength, love and support will give you what you need to reach in and help others in their time of need. For now, take a moment to celebrate a victory.

You've got this.

Love, Micah

Internalized Transphobia, Shame and Self-Hatred

Written By Lillith Campos

When it was suggested to me that I write about my own internalized transphobia I readily agreed to the task, yet inside, I had no idea how to even write this. We know what transphobia is and most of us know what internalized transphobia is as well. I think it's safe to assume that if you are transgender that you've experienced your own form of internalized transphobia. I did not know however, that cis people could experience it as well. But alas, it is true. As you read this, think about the things you've seen, heard or experienced that has shed a negative perception on the transgender community. You very likely automatically think of a man in a dress, not a woman in a dress, and that is a form of internalized transphobia. I can only speak from a transgender woman's perspective here since those are my experiences. Usually in the media or in your workplace jokes it is the transgender woman that's the spotlight. Transgender men I would think experience this as well, my own eyes just haven't been open to it yet. We, the women, are the ones typically targeted by bathroom bills, seen as predators towards children or rapists towards women in the far-right thinking community. As much as you try to let that roll off your back, part of you holds on to that and it created this self-doubt, this self-loathing inside of you. In my research for this I've read many articles and stories and my eyes were opened to things I already knew but couldn't vocalize, but I also came across a couple of new (to me) terms I'd like to explore as well. One of which is 'imposter syndrome' the feeling that you are a fraud, that you don't deserve whatever it is you have. Usually, it's linked to positions of employment or power. Yet I think it fits well in the transgender community. Myself for instance, I don't think I get to call myself a woman, I think I am a fraud. There are many reasons for those beliefs, upbringing, social interactions amongst peers, media portrayals, truscum and even TERF rhetoric.

These are very dangerous ideologies because in the TERF rhetoric you're being reduced to your ability to procreate. If you can have a period and bear children, then you're a woman. If not, regardless of transition, surgeries, lived experiences, you're a man or as the like to call us TIM's, Trans Identified Males. The very thing that feminism is fighting against, the worth of someone based off their genitals, is the very thing that TERFS use to separate us. They believe that because we didn't grow up as women, that we weren't socialized as women but instead forced to try and fit in as a man for our own safety or because we didn't have the lived experience as women then we could never truly be women. Or in the truscum rhetoric, you must have dysphoria to be transgender. More of their beliefs are of the mind you must be on HRT, actively seeking genital surgery as well else you really aren't transgender. This is especially damaging because it comes from within our community. We're experiencing gatekeeping from our own people. Not everyone can afford hormones or surgeries and that's damaging to those of us that can't. It plants that seed of doubt that we are in fact not authentic. Not all of us choose or desire to have surgery, not all of us want to take hormones or even socially transition. For some of us, just saying we are transgender is simply enough and that's ok. Regardless of where you fall within your own transition, regardless of what you choose to do or not do, you are beautiful and valid.

The other term I came across is more of a definition and it's going to challenge (hopefully) our use of the word phobia. Misia (pronounced "miz-eeya") comes from the Greek word for hate or hatred, so similar to how Islamophobia means "fear of Islam," the more accurate Islamomisia means "hatred of Islam." The definition of phobia is "an extreme or irrational fear of or aversion to something." Which was later expanded to include homophobia, transphobia, Islamophobia and so on. Which in turn expanded the definition to include "dislike of or prejudice against". And while we are all used to the term transphobia, it has brought out the sheer ignorance in people with the arguments of "I'm not scared of transgender people or of homosexual people." Basically, letting people be hateful while using the very basic definition of phobia as an example of how they aren't hateful. When in actuality what they are showing us is transmisia. A hatred towards transgender people. Will it catch on? Doubtful. But I challenge those that read this to use that term, learn new terminologies and try to spread that awareness amongst their circles and hopefully we can start calling out that behavior for what it is, hate speech.

Much like how we use identity in how we describe ourselves. That is harmful as well and we should challenge that. Do I identify as a woman or am I a woman? Do you hear cis women say they identify as a woman? No, they simply are women. It also leads to the old and invalidating statements such as "I identify as an attack helicopter" "I identify as rich or skinny", it gets old hearing those things and they are invalidating statements so we should stop them when we hear them, and we should adapt every day and open ourselves up to the personal growth that benefits not just ourselves but our community as a whole. I am a woman, and I won't stand for transmisic behavior.

So, in all my reading and reflecting on things that could cause internalized transphobia/transmisia you read about others experiences and you think back to events in your life that caused you internal shame. Maybe you didn't realize it then, but you more than likely internalized that, and it can play a part on how you see yourself. Think about this. How many of us experienced parental or familial disapproval? Bullying at school or the workplace? Or even intimate partners that engage in power and control tactics? Maybe this wasn't experienced firsthand but you’ve seen this behavior happen to someone else for being different and you see it so much that in your mind its normalized behavior, you think that if you're different that's just how you should expect to be treated. Or you turn those behaviors in on yourself and you become your own worst critic all the while accepting that behavior from others in your life. Maybe you don't correct someone when the deadname you. Maybe you don't correct someone when they misgender you. By not standing up for ourselves, we are enabling that behavior. We are showing others that it's ok to be mistreated. But it's not ok. It's damaging not only to oneself but to the entire community.

Many transgender people, particularly those who declared or displayed their gender non-conformity when young, have been subjected to years of messages that something is wrong with them, that they are unlovable, and that their gender identity will bring them lifelong pain and hatred. Not surprisingly, some of us grow up believing that ANY relationship is better than no relationship at all, and therefore, they stay in unhealthy relationships. I had the chance to come out when I was 14. It was 1990 and my mom had found my stash of girls' clothes on more than one occasion. Numerous talks and lectures didn't stop the behavior. There was no internet like there is today, there was no information out there. What was known is what was seen on the daytime talk shows of that time. Drag queens or talk shows where the man comes out as a woman in such a ridiculous charade of a woman whole the audience laughs at them. Is that what people think of me? TV shows or Movies that portrayed a transgender woman, we were always the butt of a joke and made to sympathize with the man and not the poor woman who was just exposed and laughed at. Shows, movies, those were ways that I started to develop my own internalized transmisia. I didn't even know the words at the time, I didn't even know that transition was possibly, that it was something I could ever hope to achieve but already my own internal shame was forming and at fourteen when I had the chance I chickened out and did everything I could to hate that woman inside of me that was screaming to be let out.

You see, I was sent to a psychiatrist. This is when the AIDS epidemic was still at its peak and it was illegal to be gay in most places. It was bad enough that someone was gay, but you find someone that wanted to transition? That wanted to walk away from "being a man" and live authentically as a woman? That's a cardinal sin. Men are perceived to be the top of the food chain, why would you walk away from that? Sadly, it's still like that today, just not as widespread. So, I see this psychiatrist, I already know I'm in trouble otherwise why am I going? I'm asked if I'm gay. No, I'm not. Well, am I a transvestite? No, plus I didn't know what that meant. Do you want to be a woman? Was I even allowed to say yes? The answer was no. I was scared. I still regret that answer but I've since learned it was for the best. So we continued with our sessions and determined that my behaviors were not normal. Normal is what everyone else was and I was not. Back to the closet we go for the next 26 years. Anytime a boy would do something seen as not manly he would be told to toughen up or called a sissy or called a girl. Why is being called a girl an insult anyways? Does this patriarchal misogynistic society detest women that much? Don't cry, boys don't cry. All those things you internalize. We think of ourselves as less than. As not deserving. And maybe that spills over into relationships. Some of us end up in emotionally or physically abusive relationships. And we justify being treated like that because we are different, who could really love us? We think that this is as good as we can ever hope for because we are different, less desirable. It stews and it grows and you loathe yourself for being different. But isn't being different beautiful? Why follow the masses? Follow your own path. Always be true to yourself.

I was ashamed of myself, my identity, my desires, my inner person. They crucify people like me. It would have been nice to know that I wasn't a freak and that there were others like me. But when they asked me what my problem was in school they always assumed I was just a bad kid. Little did they realize I couldn't stand myself. And hated what I was. I felt I needed to be bad to be respected and left alone. Internalized transmisia takes hold when people unconsciously absorb messages that shame, criticize, and dehumanize trans people. Overt and subtle messages that degrade or serve to exclude trans people from full participation in life are especially harmful to the transgender community. Internalized transmisia influences every trans individual differently, but it affects so many people who may not even be aware of it. We see so much transmisia around us that we might not realize how much we're carrying around internally.

Heteronormative and Cisnormative pop culture and systemic institutional practices establish ideals that rarely reflects the transgender experience, but instead provide limited depictions of how people should identify, look, and behave. And when we don't fit into that neat little box we tend to get ridiculed, again, internalizing that shame. It can manifest in the thought inside you that tells you, "You're not a REAL woman" or "You're not valid." It tells you that you're ugly, that you're not worthy of love. It tells you that the world is right to think you're disgusting. If you have a "successful" transition on the outside, you might pass as your gender to the world around you while still struggling to fight the demons within. This is why internalized transmisia is the hardest battle. It can be years after transition and you're still fighting those voices in your head, the voices that tell us why we're frauds, the voices that tell us we're just wearing costumes. It has been one of my hardest battles thus far.

But these demons can be battled, and they can be defeated. Some of us might be lucky enough to not have such demons inside themselves. But for others, knowing how to fight them is an important part of surviving in a transmisic society. Because when you are confident in your own self, the hatred of society becomes easier to withstand. You can stand regally against all the discrimination knowing that these ignorant, hateful people don't know the real you. But when you don't even know yourself, you are at risk of being twisted by society into a small, frightful person, someone who is scared of themselves and then ultimately of everything else.

This attitude of being see as "less than" has been widespread and so to finally arrive at the idea that this could be you, that YOU could be a member of this hated group can be very scary. Not only that, but by growing up in a culture and society where this attitude is common, you take it in and part of you believes it whether you want to or not. This can happen because we often learn the attitudes and beliefs of those around us before we become self-aware enough or wise enough to start questioning them. We often learn these things from trusted people around us – parents, teachers, church leaders, etc. so that we tend not to question them. We learn that a certain group of people can be mocked before we know that we are IN that group, and thus we are stuck in the position of hating something about ourselves.

Another way to fight internalized transmisia is understanding the arbitrary nature of cis normativity. Cis normativity is the idea that cis-ness is normal and being trans is freakish. And not just in a statistical sense. Clearly trans people will always be a statistical minority. But fighting cis normativity involves the idea that being trans is a normal part of human variation, like being red headed or having freckles. It's simply another way to exist that is just as valid as being cis. If we lived in a perfect society, all the negatives of being trans such as dysphoria would be nullified by affirmative therapies and we'd be able to exist without the discrimination of society teaching us to hate ourselves and causing numerous mental health problems.

In order to fight cisnormativity, it can be helpful to surround yourself with other trans humans, to soak in the beauty of the trans experience, to learn from elders who have been traveling this path for many years, who have learned to love themselves, who have fought their inner demons and won. Trans elders exist as possible models for those trans people who struggle with the question, "Is this normal?" Yes! We are normal. Our feelings are valid. We might be a rare specimen but that doesn't make us any less beautiful. For other trans people can only understand the struggles and hardships we've gone through. This is not to take away from our cis allies. On the contrary I have learned so much about womanhood from some of my closest cis allies, women who have accepted and loved me as a sister, as a best friend, as just one of the girls without so much as batting an eye. I think having a strong support system comprised of both cis and trans individuals has been what has given me the tools to battle my own internal demons.

When we understand the roots of cis normativity, we can take solace in the beauty of trans lives. Colonizing powers have erased so much trans history they have made it such that we have come to believe the lie that trans people are a recent fad. But trans history is both long and beautiful. We have always existed. Remember that. Internalize that. We have been shamans and magical people. Spiritual. Powerful. Respected. Trans humans exist in the liminal space between here and there, having made an internal journey that challenges the most powerful norms of society. There is great strength in that journey. Learn from it. Internalize it. It will be useful to fight those internal demons.

Sometimes I think I'm comfortable and confident in my identity as a trans woman, and then something happens, I "read the comments," and my internalized transmisia rears its ugly head. There's a reason they say don't read the comments. But what is it that makes us read the comments? Morbid curiosity? Myself, for some reason I think that I must suffer to earn the right to call myself a woman. But why? Why do I equate womanhood with suffering? That's misogynistic thinking that I must let go of. Because womanhood is beautiful. Womanhood is strength and solidarity. It is so many things that are kind and beautiful in this world.

Most self-destructive behaviors serve some purpose. Internalized transmisia is helping me perform my gender according to cis standards, and thus win the approval of some cis people. Society rewards trans people who pass as cis, and it punishes trans people who can't, or don't care to. This sends a clear message to trans people that cis is good, trans is bad.

On the one hand I believe it's my responsibility to eradicate my internalized transmisia—for one, because I'm responsible for taking care of myself. On the other hand, I have to be careful, because to blame myself for my internalized transmisia is a form of victim blaming. I need to be gentle with myself when I struggle, or when I'm triggered because some transmisic came out of the woodwork to remind me of all of the times I've been hurt, rejected, and made to feel inferior by cis people.

"I love you even though you're trans". When I first heard that, it brought me comfort. Peace of mind. But as time went on, I found myself questioning that phrase, you love me "even though" I am trans? What does that mean? You are not a saint because you have overlooked a "flaw" of mine, nor do I carry a flaw that needs to be overlooked. While not intended as a hurtful statement, the deliverance of this phrase still unsettles me to this day, and this mindset in the gay community is one that is a disguise for a lot of transmisia. And eventually, for me, it was one that was a disguise for my own internalized transmisia. "I love you, even though you're trans" can quickly turn into "I love myself, even though I'm trans".

For many of us, when we begin to go down the road of accepting the fact that we may be transgender, we go through a back-and-forth period of shame, self-doubt, elation, and wonder. The thought of finally being able to live as who we are is amazing. To be free of a life existing in the wrong gender and live the life we were meant to? How exhilarating that must be? But there is also a flip side, immense fear. How can I do this? Everyone will turn their back on me. I will be an outcast. What will happen with my job? These are only some of the many questions that enter our minds. Then comes the shame. How can I do this to my family? I don't want to hurt anyone and so on.

A common proposition we hear when we are questioning our gender is some sort of variation on the phrase, "If you could just press a button and automatically be any gender, what would it be?" If you could press that button, without having to deal with all the shame, pain, discrimination, loss, judgment, and bigotry, would you press it? For me it was a resounding yes, but the reality of it was that I couldn't just press a button. To be my true self, I would have to face all these things I was afraid of, but how does one do that?

When we are born, doctors assign us a gender based on our external genitalia, which is rooted in transmisia because they are basing it off the idea that men have penises and woman have vaginas. The reality is, we are who we are, and our outside appearance does not change who we are on the inside. We then navigate the world with the assumption that if a doctor told me so, then this must be true. For some of us, who we are does not match what the world has told us. But that is not always the case. We are and always have been our gender, it just may have taken us a while to affirm ourselves and who we are. Our outward appearance does not dictate and/or represent who we are. There is no one way to look: male, female, trans, non-binary, gender non-conforming and/or any other identity. Therefore, changing how we look on the outside is not a transition, just like getting a nose job, liposuction, butt implants and/or other surgeries to affirm our self-esteem are not transition surgeries. Rather, they are affirming surgeries to how we want to appear externally. Yet, when discussing these external changes regarding trans people we are so quick to label with words like transition.

When a cis person takes hormones that their body is not producing enough of, we do not label their experience as a transition. Yet when a trans person takes hormones that their body is not producing enough of, we slap on the label transition. This others trans people and again reinforces the normalcy to other trans people. If the term transition was used for everyone; trans, cis, non-binary, gender non- conforming and/or other identities, then it would not be transmisic. When a cis person changes up their style, hair, accessories, and/or other parts of themselves/identity(ies) we do not label this experience as them transitioning, when trans people do, we label it as 'transition'. Why? Why do we get othered?

All this, all this we face every day in fleeting thoughts inside our own headspace. It damages us whether we know it or not. And to hold our heads high and say, "I am enough, I am valid, and I belong", that is how we each do our own part to not only battle our demons, our internalized transmisia, but to start down the road of becoming the absolute best version of ourselves possible.

Joining My Own Chosen Family

Written By Kellen Bunting

The word community can mean so much, it's almost staggering, frankly: our town or city, our coworkers, our school peers…However, one of the most sounding and personal definitions many people carry with them exceeds any geographical connotation; a community based on one's very own identity. Being LGBT+, a recovering addict, a person of color, disabled, a veteran, part of a church…there are countless communities that can be shaped by the metaphysical standing that one has in their own life. So many differing concepts thrown together are what make you, you. And it is that very awareness that is needed to honestly appreciate why some communities cherish, and indeed thrive on, their own corner of the world.

One of the communities I look back on with great nostalgia was an online forum centered on a gay fictional romance during my middle school days. While the story itself is nothing more than wispy recollections to me today, it was the waterhole of other readers that opened my eyes to other lives, other personal journeys, other queer experiences beyond my own. I was inexplicably comforted knowing that I was not the only member of the audience struggling to hide, and later embrace, being gay. And the daily conversations around best coming out practices, other queer romance stories to check out, family situations, etc. would ultimately form my understanding that nobody is truly alone in the world. Somewhere there are people going through their own individual, but charmingly familiar, ordeals.

As I stumbled through college, I left the online communities behind and grew into communities I could embrace in-person. Most of these consisted of roommates or other friends in the residence halls, some from the jobs I worked. While I did not join any queer clubs (which I wish I had, in retrospect), I found myself nevertheless befriending plenty of other queer people around campus during my years there. And while I did not personally feel any necessity to 'reinvent myself' as so many do, I made friends and acquaintances who had. Hearing others detail their own outings and liberations eventually led me to acknowledge how privileged my life has been…

Pew Research estimates that roughly 60% of teenagers have made friends online. It would appear that "online friendships, which often form within teens' extended networks, are generally OK as long as teens balance the interactions, stay safe and realize the limitations." Perhaps one of these "limitations", from a more literal standpoint, is the awareness that one can more confidently and competently distance themselves from an online figure who rejects them for being LGBT+. After all, you don't see this person meandering down the halls of your school every day…so should you be as concerned if this wraithly presence on the other side of the monitor 'blocks' you because you came out? It is weighing of the pros and cons, the very balancing act described above between the confidence to declare yourself and hope for acceptance, and the ability to brush yourself off and move on when facing rejection.

And I remember those fears. We all do. I was scared of being an outcast. Scared of assumptions. Scared of being looked at differently. But as I got older, I become more attuned to my privileges. I began to truly understand that being adopted into a white family on a comfortable socioeconomic rung who enrolled me at a blue-ribbon school in a largely Jewish, relatively liberal New England suburb shaped an almost unfairly smooth coming out experience. Nobody cared - or if they did, it was never expressed, or made its way to me. And while it wasn't common knowledge per se, it was something about me that I'd had online in the early realms of social media for over half my high school tenure. To eventually not have actually been harassed, laughed at, ignored or avoided, bullied…how many others can say the same?

The progress much of our world has made relating to gay rights and acceptance is mind boggling. From hunting down homosexual communists to squirming at the mention of AIDS to wishy-washy Presidential candidates to future Oscar-winners showcasing the final court battles…I find it surreal. As a young man, I can vividly recall the occasional search of demographic maps online depicting the growing number of states shaded in blue representing the legality of same-sex marriage. Watching it grow from every few years to every few months was a grand catalyst to the Supreme Court working its magic and granting a generation of us the joy and relief of civil rights at work. The law's approach to civil rights is a reflection of society's approach to civil rights. And as our society has expanded the definition of civil rights, we have concurrently progressed the emotional, socioeconomic, and personal well-being of a sizable portion of our populace. With the greater emergence of LGBT+ rights being enshrined into laws, there has become a statistically significant increase in the mental health of queer youth. In fact, according to chief medical officer at the JED Foundation, Dr. Victor Schwartz, that very immersion into one's increasingly supportive community has "a protective effect in relation to suicide risk, suicidal ideation and suicidal behaviors."

I never had those thoughts, never acted on such behaviors. At least not to any tangible degree. But some who I'd met in those online forums all those years ago did. Some who I'd met in college did. After that, a couple more here and there. But while we continue to face hurdles in the news, particularly regarding the newer frontier of trans rights, we must acknowledge that overall, in the West, things have gotten better, and they can only continue to do so. We are seeing an ever-growing accepting society trying to get its arms open wider to us. The more tragic tales of LGBT+ before us are inspiring and are vital to our understanding of our own identities…but they are dwindling, and they are being replaced with stories of it making no difference to our town or city, our coworkers, our school peers, our communities of who we are. And yet ironically, I think that is the very difference we should be striving to make.

Kindness For Gregory
Written By Lillith Campos

This was written on July 12th, 2019. It was the day of my legal name change. I would wake up that morning as Greg and go to work, and that evening I would go to bed as Lillie. I would be lying if I said I wasn't nervous, not because I was unsure of myself but because I had socially transitioned only 5 weeks prior.

I spent 43 years as Greg, hiding who I was so far in the closet I was finding Christmas presents (Thanks for that line, Steph). I had no idea who Lillie was and I'm still learning who I am as a woman one year later. I was scared of the unknown and what my new role in this world would look like.

After I got home from the courthouse, with a smile on my face and tears of joy in my eyes I sat down and finished this letter. The end result you see here is nothing like my first drafts. As much as I wanted to (and sometimes still want to) hate the man I was, I have been told that I should show compassion for him. For he was doing the best he could while battling his internal turmoil in a world where women like me are seen as subhuman, he did his best to protect me. This is for you Gregory:

Dear Gregory,

There's no amount of words that can ever truly express the pain that I'm sure you've felt these years. You've kept me locked up, quiet, ignored, and worst of all - shamed for even existing. You have taken far more abuse from my internal self than is fair, even more than we have had externally. Some people have it rough in life, and you've made sure you had your fair share with your own self neglect and self-destructive tendencies.

You haven't been able to ever be yourself, because you've had to be a "boy" because of the way your body has been. I don't know if it's entirely how we were born, but there are clearly signs that we have been living behind a mask of being a man.

We may never have those answers. I will, however, live our identity as I am, not as we have been told to. That means you have to have the space to grow up and become the woman that we were meant to be, not the man that society says we are.

You have given me plenty of skills to succeed in this life and I promise I will do my best to not disappoint you as you hand off the torch to me. You have given me 4 beautiful children that I would not trade for anything in this world. I want you to know you have done an amazing job surviving in this world that can be utterly unfair and cruel at times. You plugged away and dug your heels in the ground and never gave up even though I know you wanted to.

Despite everything you dealt with and everything you were battling internally you did your best to be a compassionate human being. You struggled sometimes with your path, but you always managed to find your way through. Almost 2 years ago you started to finally listen to yourself and found me hiding inside of you and I want to thank you for that, I was starting to lose my voice. But you listened and let me start to come out. I know it has been a hell of a ride we've travelled, sometimes separately, sometimes together. Guess what? We made it. I'm proud to have had you in my life and I'm proud to have the strength you've given me to continue down this path of mine. Without you, without all your experiences in the world, this wouldn't be possible. Thank you again Gregory, I promise I'll take care of me now. I hope you will be proud while you watch me blossom into who we were meant to be.

Living with the Music

Written By Monica Furlotte

Music is the language of the subconscious. It evokes different emotions based on different notes. Lyrics can convey messages more eloquently than the spoken word. People can listen to tunes of certain vibrations to match their mood, or their life experiences. Sometimes there's just an artist, album, album cover, recommendations from others or whatever is popular that intrigues you to listen to it.

I grew up with music all around me. My parents claimed my dad placed headphones on my mom's belly to soothe me when I was kicking too aggressively. There are pictures in my family album of my first Christmas where I was only four months old. I had large headphones on my head, quizzically looking at the auxiliary cord end. I remember singing commercial bits and getting together with my cousins to create or mimic choreographed dance routines. I remember camping and bonfires where guitars were brought out, followed by strumming and Eric Clapton songs being sung into the night.

I only remember a few things of my Grampy; his rolled tobacco, his piercing blue eyes, his whiskey and him always playing the harmonica. I was told I was named after a co-worker of his, but in the back of my mind I wished it was because I was named after my grandfather's favourite instrument.

When I was growing up I spent a lot of time in libraries, record shops and garage sales, or answering ads to get new music. Hours were spent at the library in particular, where my dad would scour the selection and would pick up new albums and artists by feel. Dad had a knack at finding artists before they blew up and became mainstream. His real talent, though, was finding artists that remained underground, but made wicked sounds. Whenever we were in the car, the radio was almost never on. The exception to that was when we went on road trips, and the same old CDs would be played to the point of driving us insane. That's when CBC radio would take over and it fit the bill for us by giving us obscure, new music to listen to.

My most memorable musical experience with my dad came when I was thirteen years old. We moved to a new province, and a new school, and it was our fourth move in a year. I had just moved in with my dad. From previous experiences I knew that I was drawn to and attracted to women. This was soon common knowledge. It wasn't until I opened up about a crush on a certain paper delivery boy that my dad knew I was also into the opposite gender. I've never come across someone else who had to come out as straight or interested in heterosexual relationships before.

My dad tried to have conversations with me about my sexuality to offer support to be whoever I wanted to be. It wasn't until he handed me my first mix CD that I understood how he felt. On the way to school I started blasting his CD in my Walkman, and it was then that I started to truly feel seen. Each song, building from one to the next, was a celebration of varying expressions of sexuality like androgyny, bisexuality and all of the words and feelings I was not yet exposed to. Warmth spread throughout my body and I felt joy in my heart. A clump rose in my throat as tears poured down my face as I listened to songs from my dad that made me feel less of an alien.

Being exposed to music, celebrities, authors and other artists that shared similar lenses of seeing beauty helped me feel less alone and more connected to the world around it. It helped me better understand and actualize myself as a queer woman. As I was self-identifying as a bisexual person and meeting my first in transition trans person, I knew that binary descriptions weren't the best way to express how I love and feel attraction. Pansexuality, or being attracted to the person for their essence and not for their gender, made more sense to me than just simple bisexuality.

I remember the first few times I explained to others what that meant, and the very common response of "OOOH so you find pots and pans…sexy?" happened. It still does sometimes. I also add a yup, extra sudsy.

Nearly twenty years later, the only two songs that I remember are "One More Time" by Daft Punk and "I Do oth Jay and Jane" by La Rissa. Both songs helped me immensely in my journey in self-discovery and self-acceptance. The songs remind me to celebrate myself and that both Jay and Jane have the ability to make me feel the same kinds of happiness.

These songs and bands served as role models for me to help shape the kind of queer person that I am today. I didn't have people in my immediate community, social circle or circumstances that were part of the LGBTQ+ community, and it was important to me to find role models to help get me to a better place of accepting and understanding myself. Having these musical role models helped me build self-confidence before entering a really challenging grade nine year.

At the start of my grade nine year, we moved again, back to my home province. It meant I would be the new student again, but this time I was going back to a school I had been to before. I'd been in a relationship with someone in my grade there, things between us escalated and ended poorly between us. A girl I used to be close to was at the school and walking into the halls on that first day I heard the buzzing of curiosity about the "new" girl. Familiar faces were peering out and I could feel my dirty laundry being aired out for others to talk about. I felt like I was walking into my enemy's territory when I started to hear the words lesbian and dyke be whispered around me.

I tried to engage with different circles and social groups, never really fitting in and being picked on for the clothes I wore. I cried more often both openly and in private and was being encouraged to change in a separate stall to prevent "lesbian gazes" from making the other students uncomfortable.

A couple weeks after the move, I decided to approach an old friend. They were someone that I used to watch the clouds in the sky with back in elementary school. I timidly approached with my head hanging low and shuffling steps, I anticipated being defeated my attempt to find a friend. I asked if I could join her to eat and surprisingly, she accepted. I slowly became myself with my previous level of self-confidence. Around her I felt comfortable in being myself openly and talking a mile a minute. When I was with her it was okay to be gawking at guys and girls, chatting about the mundane parts of our lives and the hilarious things going around us.

We always picked each other for class projects, and when we were required to be in bigger groups, we would find others to join us rather than be separated. Some of those people became my lifelong friends, others are just people that I reminisce about.

There was one person in particular that saw the difference between who I was within the context of being around close friends and who I presented myself as to the rest of the school community. They picked up on how open I was to different genders and sexualities and extended an invitation to meet her other friends that were also open about their sexualities and gender expressions. I became close to quite a few members of that group back then. It felt nice to have more than one person who fully accepted me and were able to speak about sex and sexuality so openly.

I remember that the friend who invited me to their group used to debate what we learned in school with me. I always admired their feistiness and advocacy against the status quo. It was an intellectualism that I really respected in them, even when the topics they fought about are things that I can't remember anymore. One of the things I do remember us discussing that used to boil my blood was the oppression of women in the classroom, specifically the dress codes and some of the actual lessons that were taught.

I look back on that year and feel eternally grateful for the friend that accepted my invitation to eat lunch with her. We are still close friends even now that we've long graduated from high school. I'm also grateful for my other friend who introduced me to their group of likeminded individuals. We're not close anymore, but anytime I look back or bump into them in the streets I think back fondly on the friendship we had. It's comforting for me to know that he's running multiple business and is a huge pillar in the LGBTQ+ community. He's created multiple spaces for LGBTQ+ people and does LGBTQ+ sensitivity and job training.

I've been to some of the events he's put on for the community, drag shows, documentary viewings, burlesque shows, even pride events. Sometimes I'll go dancing and find that he's somehow involved in the dance production for the evening. The latest thing I've seen him in was in our local library where he was working to influence members of our city's community and provide his perspective as a transgender activist.

He created a space when I was young to be involved in, and I'm happy that he's continuing to provide safe places for the generations to come. Finding that space or creating that space really helped me feel welcomed when I was awkward and unsure of myself. He showed me that who I am deserves space as well. The ability to find inclusion regardless of one's sexuality, interests, class or learning styles is a warmth that should be cherished and chased by everyone.

I was entering singlehood at the same time I entered my adulthood. After seven year, my relationship ended and I was twenty-one years old, stumbling around wondering what to do with myself. I didn't know how to date or truly explore my sexuality. Connections I used to have with people were lost during my previous relationship, but many other connections were starting to form. One person in particular I met while dancing. Someone invited me to dance at a gay club, and it would be my first time going to a gay club in my life. I was excited, and it was a small group of people I went with. There was a timid girl who was excited to be there, but she seemed to be a bit out of place, and she was the person I was most drawn to from our group. I asked her to dance, at first, she hesitated, but she agreed and as we danced, I saw her become less self-conscious. She became more out of her head and more into her body. We danced all night and quickly became buddies. We used to go out nearly every weekend for several years, whether it was coffee or dance. Those weekend outings formed the foundation for the connection that grew between us. I slowly realized I wanted more experiences than just what I had with her and went dancing at other clubs. I made other connections and even though they were completely platonic, it felt amazing to have a space and a friend to connect to.

Over the years, I've found friendship and sexual partners in varying scenarios. I always seek connections that just allow me to express myself. I seek spaces that make me feel welcomed and safe. I am open and accepting of people from varying backgrounds and identities. The one thing I always rely on is music. It's the companion that makes me feel the most supported without seeking or needing anyone. Whenever I'm in a space or lull in my mental health, playing music that reminds me of times I had stronger connections or felt better helps me support myself through those lapses in mental health. I love myself and the journey that I've experienced. It's been more difficult lately because of the lockdowns and the inability to go to spaces or see friends, but phone calls and listening to music help me get through these harder days.

No Longer Hiding

Written By Austin Johnson

If I could reduce my childhood to a single word, it would be "lonely." I was an only child of parents who divorced at four and manifested their stress in various vices, while I created fantasy epics in my bedroom. My elementary school was the only one in our small rural community, the kind of place where everything was within a half mile of a giant convenience store in the middle of town. This was the kind of town where that same convenience store would have every flavor of vodka and Skoal available. This was the kind of place where people tossed around homophobic and transphobic slurs like they're commenting on the weather. If something or someone was "gay," it was never good. From a young age I was called a sissy, fag, or queer from bullies whether or not teachers were looking.

I quickly absorbed the message that I was an outsider and there was no safety or recourse for me even before I knew I was gay. I was always trying to be part of the group, to be a part of something, but always felt I was on the outside looking in. This developed into severe social anxiety, I was told how I "should be" as a boy when I wasn't generally into whatever the other boys were doing. I sure tried and yet I never felt truly connected to anyone- I wasn't one of the boys, and I wasn't one of the girls. It wasn't okay to be one of the girls. And so I shrank away in shame for a long time, determined to take this secret with me to the grave. The irony is, I was digging my own grave by reinforcing the shame I felt. The truth is nothing ever was wrong.

My loneliness changed abruptly in high school when I stopped hiding and came out fully within two significant days. First, I was abruptly outed by my "friend" to the entire school. Then, less than two weeks later during the middle of a two-hour drive to my mom's home after middle school graduation. The conversation went something like this.

"You're not gay, are you?" My mom asked.

I replied carefully, "No… I am."

My mom paused for about ten terrifying seconds before replying, "Oh, you mean gay like happy, right?" She asked.

"No," I said, "I mean gay like homosexual."

"Oh…" my mom replied quietly.

I told her I worried about my dad's response and I wasn't ready to come out to him and begged for her to keep it confidential. I knew my mom was terrible with keeping secrets and likely wouldn't be able to contain herself. True to form, the first thing she did when we got home was get on the phone and call my dad and the rest of the family.

I felt an anger boil within me as I drove myself mad wondering why she would do that when I had explicitly told her not to… but it didn't last long. In truth, it didn't really matter. What I mostly felt was overwhelming relief that I didn't have to keep the façade going anymore. The band-aid was ripped off… even if the wounds hadn't fully healed. I could give myself room to breathe because there was nobody left that I was keeping the secret from. A major part of my time and energy devoted to obsessing about who did and didn't know was suddenly free. Instead, I could spend all of energy doing whatever gay shit I want. And did I ever.

As a result of living openly as a gay person, the connections I made and the relationships I fostered became so much more meaningful- I was able to let loose, be more present, and really enjoy the people that were around me because they were choosing to be with me- the true me. Since coming out, I see the world through entirely different glasses- I see endless possibilities with a team behind me to help me overcome any barrier I encounter. For every asshole who tries to bash me as an opportunity to project their own self-hate and insecurity, I have three people ready to correct them and defend me without even having to do anything. I am more grateful, happy, and more fully myself which has opened the door for so much else. Sometimes, I even forget that I am different and my orientation isn't widely accepted. Because I choose my own family, friends, and the environment around me I am no longer bound by the chains of heteronormativity- though the bruises persist.

My parents each had their own fears and difficulties understanding my sexuality, but today I feel closer to them than ever. I have begun to understand that they care so deeply that it can hurt. Sometimes we externalize and project that hurt onto others as a means of connection.

It's surreal to think it has been over 16 years since I came out and reflect on just how many things I have been able to experience that I never thought could be possible. I have been married for over four years to a man who fulfills my needs in so many ways. He is an overwhelmingly positive support for me, supports my strengths and helps me push through challenges. Whose silly behavior is a panacea for when I take things too seriously. He helped me realize my path in life and encouraged me to get my Master's in social work. Now as a clinical social worker I get to share much less detailed parts of my experience to create a space of understanding and acceptance for others. Not only am I no longer hiding, but I get to help others come out of hiding themselves.

Coming out is a process that never ends, but it gets easier as you start to truly accept yourself. For me, being more and more comfortable as a queer person became a central focus of my life because it continues to affect me in so many ways. Coming out fully was one huge piece of the equation for finding my path; the other half was recognizing my ADHD and starting treatment for it. In a matter of days, thoughts were organized neatly for the first time in my life. It's like I could finally see the trees through the forest, recognize the markers I had laid out for my future self and find my path through it. As good as it was, it was still incredibly overwhelming to adjust to an entirely new self-concept.

During my own crisis of identity and the power of introspection, my thoughts were finally able to solidify, and I had clear direction. I've considered myself an artist first and foremost- and it was also how most people knew me throughout school. I was easily bored, rarely challenged in school, also desperate for more vulnerable relationships. So, I lead by example- I would do what I could to make someone's day more interesting, more enjoyable- leave a lasting positive impression, often to my own detriment. I also liked to be provocative- be unexpected and make people think about their own conceptions. Some teachers appreciated it, and I was considered a "positive influence in class. For others, it was highly inconvenient for their intricately manicured curriculum, and I was sent home with a note to my parents for "distracting the other students." Looking back, the main thing that always held me back was this unrealistic expectation that I had to perform to a strict hetero-normative code to maintain any kind of social status and acceptance. When I think about what makes my inner child full of glee, and reflecting on my own development, I reconnect with that genuine joy and passion; I am happiest when I am creating something.

By noticing the ways my truest self-found hope and joy through the trials of queer youth, I can identify the steps toward building my authentically idealized self: a comedic artist who wants to "do it all" and has grand fantasies about what they can accomplish. I've always had a natural affinity for the arts: acting, singing, dancing, fashion design, and the “fine” arts. I didn't really know other queer people, and it was hard for me to find role models that I could identify with. If anything, I found myself resonating with strong, smart, and value-driven women who dominated in fields that weren't designed for them. Also, ones who were multi-talented and breathtaking just to look at.

With the mainstream exposure of RuPaul's Drag Race, I got to learn deeply about drag artists and their sources of inspiration, who in turn became my new sources of inspiration. Drag artists embody radical self-love. Queens channel the strong women who inspire them into a living expression of their entire creative being, incorporating daring and imaginative use of media into uniquely personal performances. For someone who has struggled with genuine expression even in my art, it is courageously vulnerable and awe inspiring. And when the audience erupts into a cacophony of radical queer joy, it the best sort of therapy for those of us who were ridiculed for who we are and made to suppress it. Within these shared spaces, we can truly celebrate each other's authentic selves... and I am living for it!

Playing To Win
Written By Conner Mertens

How does one compare the feeling of draining a last second three-pointer for a win? Catching the game winning touchdown in double-coverage? Sinking a forty-foot putt on the eighteenth for a win? Smashing a ball over the right field wall in extra innings? Asking an athlete to describe this feeling often evokes strong, emotionally loaded language; if the athlete is able to muster up words at all. Because in that moment...we are infinite. We are invincible. We are us. I believe in the poetic side of athletics. The raw beauty embedded in its core. Its ability to change people. Its ability to bring people together. Regardless of ideology...a field, court, course, whatever it is, it does not care about anything going on outside the moment. It is a comforting idea that for a set amount of time, nothing matters but the activity presented before you.

If you have experienced one of these speechless moments, you know how powerful and emotional of a feeling it is. Now imagine having all that stripped from you because of the gender you were attracted to. Something so trivial as sexual orientation defining your ability or inability to play a sport. It is nothing short of heartbreaking to imagine someone being deprived of something so beautiful and empowering as athletics because someone is not comfortable with who they are.

My name is Conner Mertens, and I am the first active college football player to come out as LGBT at any level. In this process, I made my contact information available for anyone who could find it useful. All too often, the stories listed above were not a clever anecdote used to start a piece of writing, but the cruel reality for many athletes. The breakdown of people reaching out to me following my coming out was about twenty percent active athletes looking for support, twenty percent people of faith wanting to discuss that aspect and sixty percent former athletes with tales of discrimination and heartbreak. Email after email poured in with the words, "...and I forced to quit the sport I love because my team found out my sexual orientation."

So imagine, if you will, all those incredible explanations of sport from earlier being ripped away from you. Not for lack of talent or ability but because someone else does not understand you. Criminal and gut wrenching is what that amounts to.

The fact that I was able to be open about my sexuality and not hide or suppress it was inconceivable by many of these former athletes. Fortunately for me, I found some amazing outlets and resources early on that helped make the process as smooth as it could be. Getting connected to the You Can Play Project immediately gave me confidence and comfort that I would not have had otherwise. However, without my initiative to actively go out and search for support, I would not have had that outlet. There seems to be a general lack of support for the LGBTQ athlete throughout sports. Without support for the LGBTQ athlete, we will continue hearing the very real stories of individuals forced to quit their respected sport for an issue that has absolutely nothing to do with athletics. We have come leaps and bounds from Paragraph 175 in Nazi Germany and the Stonewall Riots in New York. But we still have a long way to go.

In March of 2015, I spoke to a golfer at the Division 1 level who was kicked off their team the day after they were outed by teammates. This is a shadowy reminder that these problems are not outdated nor abstract. This is a very real and very present issue that still requires our attention. I have seen the faces and heard the stories. The forceful end to one's athletic career because of their “lifestyle”. Before I go on: let's quit referring to the existence of a demographic of people as a "lifestyle". It is me. Going to the gym is a lifestyle. Having love for someone is called being human. Another one is we need to stop praising individuals for their “tolerance”. Tolerance is a small step up from hatred yet below indifference. Tolerance acknowledges that something or someone is not agreeable, but that person is choosing to see past that inherent pitfall and put up with their existence. No one wants to be tolerated. People want to be loved and accepted. I tolerate broccoli, I love people.

At the end of the day, I am just a stupid kid. Thrown into the spotlight overnight for writing a letter to my hometown, I don't know much. But one thing I know and understand is the power and liberation behind the ability to simply be yourself. Friends from across all walks of life and demographics, take heed and hear these words (I've always wanted to say that) ...they may even change your life. If you take nothing from my words, understand this: Bust out of that cage of oppression called insecurity and realize you were put on this earth not just to survive, but to thrive and be the best version of yourself. And above all else, know that hope is everywhere. You just have to know the right places to look.

I will leave you with this one simple question: Are you happy? Are you happy with what you are doing in this life? Are you living your life for yourself or for someone else? Have you lost track of who you are because it was easier being someone else? It took me many years to realize my own answer to these questions. I came out to one to one of my closest friends and they told me that I had given them the courage to finally tell that girl that he liked her. That's what this is about. Being real with yourself and others. If you like to dance, get jiggy with it. If you like to sing, get your Justin Timberlake on. If you like to box, go get 'em, Rocky, if you like that girl, what's holding you back, Romeo. Point is, don't let society dictate who you can and cannot be simply because it doesn't fit their perception of who you are supposed to be.

Pride Speaks

Written By James Sanyshyn

I was born in 1969, a benchmark year for LGBTQ rights. Pierre Elliott Trudeau, when introducing legislation to decriminalize homosexuality famously said: "…The state has no place in the bedrooms of the nation." The Stonewall riots showed that the LGBTQ community had had enough of the intimidation, harassment and extortion they faced even in America's most progressive city.

Not that Stonewall made a difference in rural southern Alberta in the 1970's. As a child, I was told to "walk like a man", "speak more masculine", sent for full psychiatric and physical exams, and taught that perverts burned for all eternity. I share this not to blame my family or faith as they all wanted me to be saved from myself from an inevitable and ugly future of bullying, harassment and violence.

Surviving high school was a daily challenge. Having a "girlfriend" was good cover for a while. It even got me through my Canadian Armed Forces interview to join the reserves in 1989. "Do you have a girlfriend?" "No." "Have you ever had a girlfriend?" I could live with a feeble yes. In 1992, as a result of court losses, the Canadian Armed Forces reversed its policy of discrimination and lesbians and gays could now serve their country without lying about their sexual orientation.

Coming out to best friends was harrowing, but total acceptance was the response. My mother was trying to "out" me by raising Ellen DeGeneres' coming out on TV in 1997, by speaking about the gay couple on her block, and by asking me about my pierced ear. Sadly, her attempts to help me love and accept myself with family were cut short by her sudden passing. Her loss rocked our family and kept me in the closet for two more years.

The letters I wrote to family, small town folk with religious backgrounds, were accepted with unconditional love by all. My fears were allayed, and I learned about acceptance from those closest to me. My dad's voice mail: "Hi, it's your Dad. I got your letter. I can't say that I'm surprised. I want you to know that this doesn't change anything for me. You're my son and I still love you. OK, talk to you later. Bye." Short, sweet, tears of relief.

As a gay teacher, I was drawn to GALE BC, the Gay and Lesbian Educators of BC, who in 1999 were assisting in the fight against the Surrey School Board ban of same-sex family books. James Chamberlain became a mentor and friend and risked so much for a just cause: to allow students, staff and parents to be exactly who they are, without compromise and without retribution. He and others taught me to be loud and proud! It was through that fight and subsequent fundraising events that I met my former husband. We were engaged just as same sex marriage came to British Columbia in 2003 and were among the first 10 couples married here upon the change of law. We fought over who got to cross out the title "bride" from the marriage license as the new forms had yet to be printed!

My principal at the time was noticeably uncomfortable reading this piece of "good news" during our staff meeting as scripted by me: "Another piece of good news…silence, coughs. We have a summer wedding to announce. James and Lyle were married in July – congratulations." Whispers. "Did he say Lyle" "Sounds like a guy." The Language department threw me a party and gave me champagne! Despite the awkward announcement, nothing came my way but love and acceptance. I felt so incredibly blessed.

In 2004 I started the GSA at Burnaby South. I was nervous and concerned that students might be the target of bullying. I had excellent support from my principal, who is now superintendent. The RCMP liaison officer was made aware of the meeting time and location. We ordered pizza and were delighted that seventy students showed up! We managed to hold onto thirty to forty students after that for several years and our GSA is still going strong with other sponsor teachers today.

Not being satisfied, I and other long-time activists, such as Debra Sutherland, decided to present to the Burnaby Board in 2009 regarding a distinct LGBTQ policy for our district. Our initial request was rebuffed by trustees with the usual "we deal with all bullying the same way." Undeterred, our little group began lobbying and organizing to effect positive change. I had the full support of the Burnaby Teachers Association and British Columbia Teachers' Federation. Student voices were too compelling to ignore, and many chose to attend to explain why this policy was so important. I was so proud of them as they spoke before the Board, which could only change its mind years long process.

The work of policy writing continued, out of the media, without controversy. That is, until the draft of the policy was released to district parent advisory council. Almost overnight, hundreds protested with signs, counter delegations presented, death threats were sent, a single-issue political party was born…yet, our trustees, staff students and supportive parents and allies did not back down. Our policy passed and became the 13th in British Columbia. Our voices are at the table now. Our district walks the walk with regulations and a dedicated part-time diversity consultant teacher. We march in the Pride Parade. We also attend conferences and an annual Gender Sexuality Alliance International Day against homophobia breakfast.

My life is not unique; rather, it has paralleled a movement of suppressed, repressed and targeted individuals rising up for themselves and future generations of their own. I am so proud to tell my story, as it is interwoven with the stories of countless others, under one ever expanding rainbow.

Queer Taboos

Written By Lillith Campos

This has been a long time coming, needing to be put down, both for my own mental health and the mental health of others. Living in the internet age has put vast amounts of knowledge at our fingertips, both for the good and the bad. More and more people have accesses to resources now that we didn't have when I was growing up. As a teenager if I needed to know how to fix something on my car, I had to refer to the repair manual. If I was unfamiliar with a certain subject, I would look it up in an encyclopedia. In today's world it is easy to just google what you're looking for and it's right there on a screen in front of you. I grew up in a small military town some would consider out in the country. Compared to how it's grown up since then I guess they were right. I always thought it was a city, maybe not big city scale but I knew it wasn't no one stoplight town. I was fortunate in that we had a somewhat culturally diverse community, but LGBTQ was still taboo and underground. Growing up confused about my gender, confused about my anger, I had no such resources. These were taboo subjects. I was coming of age at the end of the height of the AIDS epidemic and I remember it being called the gay disease. If anyone got AIDS, they were assumed to be closeted gay. We were so naive back then about so many things in the world. You could be sent to a psychiatrist to 'cure' you of your crossdressing because being a transvestite (terminology at the time) is immoral.

In today's world it's easier for us to connect with each other and find out that we are, in fact, not alone in this world. That would have saved so many lives when I was growing up. But along with the ease of accessing such communities and information comes the bad things. Bullies will always be bullies, only now they are bolder than in the past: they get to hide behind a keyboard and suffer no real consequences. It's easier to be stalked, people set up accounts with the sole intention of outing people who aren't out yet to friends and colleagues. But all is not lost. I tend to believe in the good in humanity and have found many examples of that. Online support groups for whatever you need support with are out there. All you have to do is google it. Maybe there isn't anyone near you that's going through the same thing or likes the same things you like, but somewhere out there online there is.

I found such friendship not too long ago in an online support group for Anxiety, Depression and Suicide. What brought me to search for such a place was the fact I am transgender. I was AMAB and I am now living authentically as a woman. Up until I started questioning my gender, my very core of my being, I led a tormented life. I could never pinpoint what it was, yet I always knew something was amiss. I had dabbled in crossdressing most all of my life and I often had wished for a magic lamp or the ability to shape shift into the body of a woman. Initially I would think, if I could just have a few days as a woman and that changed into a 'Please, just give me an hour to experience womanhood'. I longed to carry a baby and give birth, I longed for menstrual cycles as well. Those thoughts or periods of crossdressing were always followed by guilt. I was a man and I wasn't supposed to have such thoughts. I did the only thing I could think to do, I practiced hyper masculinity.

This cycle led to many depressive episodes and I would always do my best not to let it show because I was a man. You can't be bothered by such things when you're a man. It's a sign of weakness.

This cycle of who I am at my very core trying to come out to myself followed by shame followed by hyper masculinity would continue for close to 30 years until I met Nova. Nova is my therapist and from the beginning she assured me that I am valid. No matter what I do in life, I am valid. I could transition or not transition. She showed me that there is no real black and white when it comes to life and being transgender in particular. I often say that the best and worst day of my life was when I met Nova. Finally, there was a light at the end of the tunnel for me. Finally, I had hope, maybe I could even experience happiness one day. Yet exploring your gender and coming out as transgender presents a whole new set of problems that most in this world will never deal with. The sheer amount of strength it takes to live authentically is exhausting. You are constantly thinking about your presentation. Is this or that going to get me clocked? Am I walking correctly? Am I talking correctly? Am I sitting right? You're constantly worried about your safety. Are those people laughing at you or did someone tell a joke? Are people just humoring you to your face and talking differently behind you back? Will this place be friendly to transgender people? Is this place safe?

I had male privilege and like most I thought that was a myth. Something people say just to invalidate your opinion. Well, I'm here to tell you that when you lose that place of privilege as a cishet white male you become painfully aware of the privilege you had. You're seen as an abomination, a man playing dress up in my case. Most men look down on you for abandoning manhood. It's the peak of evolution after all so why would you want to give that up? I would say most of us lose relationships, friends, family members and that leads to more depression on top of your feelings of inadequacy and dysphoria. People constantly use the wrong pronouns, some accidentally and some intentionally citing that they always knew you as (deadname) and you'll always be that person. Those little micro aggressions hurt, and the onus is on you to not be offended at the offender because they really didn't mean it.

I think that most of us in the LGBTQ community experience depression at least once in our lives. Some of us are better equipped to cope with it, maybe in the form of a support system or hobbies and activities. Some of us don't have a support system or we just don't know how to deal with it. And sometimes when we are in these depressive episodes our mind starts messing with us. Like a little voice whispering in your ear. 'Maybe you're better off dead.' 'Stop being such a burden to everyone.' 'They would be better off without me.' Those thoughts quickly snowball into more and more dark thoughts. Maybe we self-harm in an attempt to alleviate the pain we are feeling inside. Maybe we engage in dangerous activities that have an increased risk of death, after all, you can't say I committed suicide if I was just speeding, driving recklessly and got in an accident and passed away. The more depressed you get the darker these thoughts are sometimes. You long for death, you romanticize it, it's all you can focus on, you see it as the ultimate act of self-love.

You can't talk to anyone about it though because mental health still has a stigma attached to it. Suicidal thoughts and suicidal ideation even more so. When you try to bring it up to someone you see the way they look at you differently or worse yet, they make your pain about themselves. 'But I'll miss you.' 'What will I do without you?' One of my favorites 'Stop being so selfish, you're only thinking about yourself, and you need to think about the people you would leave behind. It would break our hearts.' Maybe I was thinking about everyone and removing the burden that I am from your lives. Those things are not things you should ever say to someone battling suicide. Much like the 'why can't you just snap out of it?' 'What do you have to be depressed about?' Comments one should never say when someone is battling depression.

Maybe you don't know what to say to someone battling depression or suicide and that's fine. Just don't ever belittle their experiences. Don't ever make it about you or try to minimize their experiences. Just listen. Express that you know they are hurting and just offer your ear to them. Unless you know for a fact that an attempt is imminent, don't call anyone such as LEO or EMS. Just listen. Sometimes that's what's needed to help someone. Maybe you can't relate to what they are feeling so tell them so, but also tell them at the same time that you're there for them anytime they need to vent. Tell them to give it 'X' amount of time to work through these feelings and if they're still feeling this way at that time then maybe we can look at another way work through this and discuss other options. Just be supportive, that more than anything else is what's needed.

That online support group I mentioned earlier? I joined it in December of 2019. I was in my most depressive/suicidal state I've ever been in. I had only been living fulltime as Lillie for about 6 months, I still had no ideas who I was as a woman. Things were toxic at home, and I was hurting a lot. I resorted to self-harm in the form of cutting. It allowed me to focus on that physical pain instead of the mental anguish I felt at the time. It worked briefly; I was able to bleed out my pain. I made a post in that support group about my desire to die. I talked about my life and my children and my fears of 'messing' them up for being trans as well as my fears of them not wanting anything to do with me as they got older or seeing me as an embarrassment for being trans. I thought they would be better off without me instead of being picked on because dad is now a woman. I hated being transgender, I still do, to a point. Yet at the same time, looking back on my life, I can say for a fact I am happier than I've ever been in my life. Funny how that works.

I got the support one would expect from a support group even though most could not relate to the transgender experience. Two people stood out in the responses though. Rose and Emily. Both transgender women who were suffering as well. We started our own little group chat and bonded quickly through our pain and shared experiences as transgender women. It would be equal parts building the others up or venting your own frustrations. Often, we would talk of our attempts, what we thought we did wrong, how we would do it, always looking for that guaranteed way to end it. We once signed a e-contract between the three of us to not kill ourselves on a month-to-month basis. The contract would be renewed monthly. It only made it one month. I was climbing out of my hole thanks to my therapist, my doctor and two of my best friends over a period of some serious intervention, crying and opening of my soul from a Thursday through the following Monday. Details of which are known only to those closest to me.

I credit those women with saving my life. They might say I'm the strong one or that I did all the hard work and maybe one day I can acknowledge that. Today, they get all the credit for listening to me, for helping me and comforting me in my time of need.

So that contract, I didn't see a need personally to renew it on my end, yet I would have been more than happy to resign it. Emily had just come out of a stint of inpatient therapy and was telling us she was doing a lot better. Rose was still struggling but wouldn't sign the contract since we didn't 'need' it like she did. Yet we still spoke daily. I continued to improve and was still scared at how bad off I was before and how close I was to my own inpatient stay. I was too close to death and even though I thought that's what I wanted at the time, when I was standing on the metaphorical cliff, I found that's not what I wanted to do. I have had this happiness since then at beating my demons. It's only been 4 months since then and I'm still riding a high I hope never goes away.

Rose has struggled the whole time and I've worried for her so. Emily would have cycles of happiness and depression. We all three continued to talk, continued to check on each other. Emily had an attempt at hanging herself that failed and another attempt at an OD that left her having seizures and in the ER, followed by another inpatient stay. Emily hated the fact she wasn't born cis and would never have the experiences of a girl growing up. She suffered more when people used the wrong pronouns or disowned her for being transgender. She would tell us that she wanted to try to hold out until her debt was paid off from all her medical bills from her attempts before killing herself so her family wouldn't be stuck with her debt.

Even in pain she would not let me feel inadequate as a parent for being transgender. She cared deeply about others, just not her own life. She never liked to see anyone else hurting and would always check on us, especially if we were suffering. On 4/20/2020 she succumbed to her pain and depression and killed herself. It shook me to my core because that could have easily been me- it was so very close to being me. I was in the process of writing my goodbye letters when my therapist told me it was probably time to go to inpatient. She had been trying to help me intensely for close to two months and I was just getting worse. I was to follow up with my doctor and come back on Monday and see what route was going to be taken. Driving to my doctor on the Saturday after seeing my therapist I drove by where my best friend lived and reached out to her on a whim and asked her to come to the doctor with me.

She knew of my struggles before but this time I kept most of it from everyone. So she sat with me at my doctor for hours while we talked and we all cried and I was able to get a lot of my pain out. Come Monday I was doing so much better, so much weight was lifted off my shoulders. Were it not for that experience over the weekend, I wouldn't be here now to write this. Once I had finished my goodbye letters to those important to me, that was it, I was going to end it. I was so close. It could have been me. That's part of why it hit me so hard to find out about Em's. Because it could have been, it nearly was me.

I was initially mad at Emily. We had this agreement between us that if it got so bad that we were going to end our life we would call or reach out via text to the other two and say goodbye and give the other two a chance to say goodbye. We wouldn't try to stop them, just say goodbye. That idea came from another best friend who told me to give her that much if I chose to end it. I think the idea of calling and saying goodbye is a good idea because you're voicing your actions out loud to someone, you're hearing your own voice say goodbye and that would hopefully give you pause and not go through with it. I think that's what my bestie had in mind when she told me to at least give her the chance to say goodbye.

Emily did not say goodbye however and being hurt I turned to anger. Initially at Em's for not saying goodbye, but that anger soon turned towards suicide itself and how we as humans get to that point in our lives. You never can fully know the impact you can have on someone’s life. I am visibly trans and I have a deep voice. I'll never pass and yet I'm happy. So when others say 'ma'am' 'Ms.' use she/her pronouns or even start off with 'girl let me tell you....' those things fill me with such joy. Or when you're included in conversation or activities for your authentic gender it means the world to me. Small, what seems like insignificant acts of kindness and human decency makes all the difference in the world. Sometimes its those small acts that can actually save a life. Some of you may never know how something so small such as the wrong pronoun can cut someone to their core.

Think about all those times you've put your foot in your mouth or even made what you thought was an innocent comment. That woman you said looks like death warmed over? She just lost her baby. Your coworker who seemed out of it today and you told him to stop daydreaming and focus on his job? His dad just passed away. We have no idea what other people are going through. Maybe your best friend is struggling financially, on the verge of losing their home and can't go out for drinks but you tell them to stop being a prude. We don't know what others are going through and the burden is not on them to tell us their troubles so we will be nice to them. The burden is on us to be kind and decent human beings and in doing so you just might save a life. Be especially kind to those in the LGBTQ communities because every day for most of us we have to live in fear of violence towards ourselves. Ask their pronouns. Do not ask their preferred pronouns as that indicates we have a choice. We chose to live as who we always were. We chose to drop the facade that came with our assigned gender. Be especially kind to people of color as they have suffered more than any of us can possibly understand. Just be kind.

I can't tell you how important it is to be able to talk candidly about suicide and depression. There were many times my best friend would listen to me while we were on break at work or eating lunch together. She would just listen and never once showed an ounce of judgement. Or another dear friend would listen to me at night over the phone or via text. She would drop whatever she was doing at that moment and give me her undivided attention and when she herself was struggling I would do the same for her. We have to be able to talk about this and not just in a clinical session but also amongst our friends and loved ones. That's why it's so important to just listen. You never know how close someone is to ending it and you could be the reason they stayed alive we all have the ability to be heroes.

And if you're ever struggling yourself then please reach out to someone you can trust. Anyone at all. Your life is too precious to throw away. Reach out to your local support groups or any online support groups. You can always call the National Suicide Prevention Lifeline at 1-800-273-8255 or go to https://suicidepreventionlifeline.org

The Trans Lifeline at 1-877-565-8860 or go to https://www.translifeline.org

Help is there, the resources are there, all we have to do is reach out. All we have to do is be kind. Kindness can stop these senseless deaths. Please, for all the Emily's out there, practice love and kindness.

Emily Brown 5/26/1994 - 4/20/2020 I hope you found your peace and your happiness. You will be missed. I love you.

Recollections

Written By Alex Keen

It is 2008, I am 17 years old, and I have just been outed in front of my family.

My dad has his head in his hands. His shoulders are shaking silently. I am frozen in place.

My mother is staring at me, horrified, tears in her eyes. I do not know what to do.

My fifteen-year-old brother is gobsmacked. I am utterly unprepared for this moment.

My sister, aged 9, is looking from face to face, trying to work out what is happening. I have no words to explain this.

"What?" says my brother. "No, seriously, is this a joke? This is a joke, right?" He looks to my mum. He looks to my dad. He turns his stare back to me.

I shrug helplessly.

It is 2002, I am 11 years old, and I feel very weird.

There are a lot of boys around me. Somehow, this is something I am very aware of all of a sudden. I notice them in a way I didn't, and I am not sure when I started noticing them.

Of course, I've always known that boys exist, and so does every other boy around me, I am sure. But now, I have realised something nobody else seems to see: boys have bodies.

When I am sat at a desk, my attention is drawn to the back of the neck of the boy in front of me. I imagine reaching out and touching the soft downy hairs that stray below the close-cropped cut. In the library, I look at the legs tucked under chairs and, as my eyes rise up, dare to contemplate what lies beneath the zips. During lunchtime, when we are lining up to enter the dining hall, the disordered queue often becomes a press, and I am electrified by the arms that press against mine.

Twice a week, I have to go into a room with all the other boys and take off my clothes. It is beyond comprehension that everyone else seems fine with this. Here, and only here, is it acknowledged that there is the possibility that some boys might look at other boys in the way that I want to look, and it is universally agreed that doing so—wanting to do so—would be shocking, laughable, wrong.

Despite my attempts to hide my eyes, the glimpses of brightly coloured underwear invade my dreams each night.

It is 2004, I am 13 years old, and I am alone.

My bedroom is dark. My back is pressed against the wall, half-undressed, headphones playing gentle piano music in my ears. Suddenly, I am seized by a sense of loss. I want to curl up into a ball and cry.

I want to be held. I want another boy, someone like me, to hold me in his arms. To stroke my hair and press me close, hot, with his breath on my neck, hold me so tight it hurts, and I still ache to be closer. I can picture him, chest hard, sweat tart, shoulders broad, voice an echo of my own, body a sponge for my loneliness. I can feel the tears pressing the inside of my scrunched-up eyes.

I imagine a boy. Today, the boy has curly brown hair and blue eyes. He is broad-chested, a little taller than me. His name is Luke. He has a grin on his face. We are lying in grass.

Yesterday the boy was a redhead. He was skinny and sad. I rested my chin on his head as he buried his face in my neck. We met in a sandy cave on the edge of a beach. His name was Ryan.

Tomorrow the boy will be different, and the day after. My teachers have always said I have a powerful imagination. Sometimes we are just talking, sometimes we play-fight, sometimes we kiss. Sometimes, we touch each other. More than anything, though, we hold one another. Each night, I can almost feel the boy in my arms.

In all these fantasies, the boy and I are always in private, always alone. Of all the things I can imagine, I can't consider the idea of our fragile, perfect moment together surviving the trauma of being seen.

It is 2006, I am 15 years old, and I am suffocating.

I am sat in the front passenger seat of my mum's car. We are waiting at a traffic light, the song that was playing on the radio has just finished and now we are sat in silence.

My tongue feels sticky in my mouth. My hand is white on the seatbelt. All the air in my lungs is pressing against the inside of my vocal cords.

"I like boys. I don't like girls. I am gay. I like men. I love men. I've been having these thoughts about guys. I want to date a guy. I want to date guys. I like guys. I think I'm gay. I know I'm gay."

This is what I don't say. I've been rolling the phrases around on my tongue for weeks, and I'd even managed to convince myself that it was purely speculative, imagining what it might sound like if I were for some reason to come out. Casual. Inconsequential. Just an offhand thought that I keep on having for no particular reason, like you do.

Now, suddenly, sat at this traffic light, I am crushingly aware of how hard the words are fighting to get out, and how terrified I am of saying them.

My mum is a psychotherapist. She has shelves upon shelves of books about tolerance, and acceptance, and love. She has a gay brother. She has gay friends. When I was 9 or 10, she gave me a book about how some boys like girls, and others like boys, and some girls like boys, and others like girls, and some people like both, and how all of that is okay. She has told me and our brother and sister out loud, together and individually, many times on separate occasions, that she and my dad will always love us, no matter what we do, no matter who we are, no matter who we love.

So why can't I say it?

The light changes. A new song comes on the radio. I exhale. My mum asks me a question I don't hear. It is an ordinary day.

Alphabet of Hope

It is 2007, I am 16 years old, and I cannot believe the words that are coming out of my mouth.

I am in the office in our house, talking to my mum, telling her I have something to say. I have realised that I cannot wait for the right moment. If I try to plan for the right moment, I will chicken out. I will never be ready, and I can't wait any longer.

So I trick myself into it. Here's how I do it. I walk into the room, and I open my mouth and I say "Mum".

Now she's looking at me. I have to say something. She will know something is wrong if I don't say something.

"What is it?"

"I have something to tell you."

Great. Now she can tell that this is isn't just a random thing, it's *something*.

I am trembling with the effort of keeping my mind blank, not letting myself come up with a lie. Not letting myself imagine what will happen next.

"Okay… You can tell me anything."

"I… am…"

Breathe.

"I'm gay."

Several months later, we're sat at the dinner table. My brother and I, eager for anything to talk about other than ourselves and school and our teenage selves, are loudly contemplating a brochure that the family received, explaining all the things we can do with the reward points my mum has accrued from shopping at a nearby supermarket, with running commentary from our parents and our little sister.

"We could get a half price subscription to a monthly wine club!"

"You don't even like wine, and they're always half off anyway. Ooh, they sell Nerf guns—"

"No! No toy guns in my house, thank you."

"Fine. How about a hot tub?"

"Like with bubbles? I'd like a hot tub in the garden."

"Do you know how long those things take to fill up? And then you have to clean them every time you use them. And we get so many leaves in the garden."

"We could go on a cruise. I've always wanted to go on a cruise."

"Yeah, a GAY cruise!"

The world freezes.

"Why would it be a gay cruise?" asks my mum. She has been encouraging me to tell them for months. I am waiting for the right moment.

My brother cracks an excellent joke: "Because Alex is gay, duh."

“Well I’m glad he's told you, but let’s not make jokes like that please.”

It is 2008, I am 17 years old, and I have just been outed in front of my family.

My dad has his head in his hands. His shoulders are shaking silently. I am frozen in place.

My mother is staring at me, horrified, tears in her eyes. I do not know what to do.

My fifteen-year-old brother is gobsmacked. I am utterly unprepared for this moment.

My sister, aged 9, is looking from face to face, trying to work out what is happening. I have no words to explain this.

“What?” says my brother. “No, seriously, is this a joke? This is a joke, right?” He looks to my mum. He looks to my dad. He turns his stare back to me.

I shrug helplessly.

My mum is on the verge of crying. “Oh Alex, I’m sorry! I thought you’d told him! I’m so sorry! Oh my god, Alex, I thought you'd told him!" She remains in this loop for at least a minute.

My dad is actually crying, tears of laughter streaking down his face.

My sister says, "Is there someone you're being gay with?" When I shake my head, she asks how I know I'm gay. My mum, who has recovered somewhat, explains that I like boys and not girls.

"Oh. Okay then." She goes back to eating her peas.

My brother looks at me dumbfounded.

"Erm, sorry?"

"It's okay. I probably would like to go on a gay cruise."

And it was that easy.

It is 2009, I am 18 years old and today is my first day at university. We are sat around, getting to know one another, relying on cheap lager and the structure of I Have Never to compensate for the fact that we are all terrified that everyone else is an adult and we are not.

Someone says, "I have never kissed a guy." I take a deep breath, and a quick swig. I say, out loud, to nobody in particular, "I'm gay." Then I shrug and take another swig.

Each time I say it, the heartbeat pounding in my chest is a little more manageable.

It is 2018 and I am old enough that when someone asks me how old I am, I have to think about the answer. I'm sat in a pub with my sister, who has somehow become old enough to have opinions on global politics as she gesticulates with a glass of Sauvignon Blanc in her hand. I ask her whether she's joined any societies at university.

"Well, there's a cheese and wine society, which obvs I wanted to check out, but they had like a hundred and fifty people sign up at the fresher's fair and the student union are at war with the Uni over whether they can even stay open or whether it's encouraging drinking, which I think is stupid because students drink anyway and it's not like a glass of wine and a couple of slices of cheese is doing more harm than £1 pints at the End of Exams party, is it? So, there's that, and the film society, and Politics Society because you basically have to be on the committee for your course society if you want to run for student council, and the LGBT society."

She throws me a little glance.

"Oh yeah?"

"Yeah, I'm bisexual."

"That's cool."

"Thaaanks. Can I have another glass of wine please?"

My heart is bursting with pride.

Showing Up

Written By Trevor Ritchie

It's a cliché to say that coming out is a process that never ends. I'm coming out right now actually. My name is Trevor Ritchie and I'm gay. Saying that, or writing it in this case, gets easier the more I do it. Part of that is how comfortable I am with myself. Part of it is that society is generally more accepting; I can wear a rainbow wristband or rainbow shoelaces in public and not have anyone comment. The last part is that I've seen the whole range of responses, and nothing surprises me anymore. I've had people cry in agony, suggest I need therapy, scream in delight and even fall off furniture in surprise. Experience has made coming out easier. I didn't have the luxury of that experience growing up. That experience only came after I learned to trust people.

Baseball was a passion of mine as a kid. I loved to play, even though I was terrified of being hit by the ball. Over thirteen years of playing, being hit by the ball was an experience I repeated more times than I care to admit, despite my skills and the reflexes I developed to avoid being hit. Baseball was also a major source of anxiety for me. I wanted to continue playing competitively, but I couldn't see how the team would ever accept a gay teammate. I knew I needed to come out eventually but deciding when and how to come out to everyone was harder for me to figure out.

The question of when to come out became easy, it was the summer of 2006. The season I turned sixteen we lost every game we played, and I tore my hamstring. My baseball career hung my a few ligament threads, and if coming out caused a backlash then I had plenty of reasons to quit playing. Telling the whole team at once seemed like a bad idea. I decided to tell the incoming head coach's son. We'd known each other for years already. First as opponents and rivals from different local organizations, and then more recently as teammates that hadn't fully earned each other's respect. I also knew he went to Catholic school, so I thought he would be more likely than other teammates to have a bad reaction, and I could gauge how the rest of the team would react based on what he said and did.

We decided to go golfing at a local pitch and putt course to figure out how we could have some success in the following season. Neither of us wanted a repeat where we lost every single game. We had a lot of time to talk about it as well, our round of golf was taking much longer than it should have because of how badly I was playing. As it turns out, baseball skills are not fully transferable to golf. Hitting a moving baseball is an entirely different set of skills than hitting a much smaller, stationary golf ball. Being extremely anxious probably didn't help my game either. We had only gotten halfway through our game when Alex suggested we finish up and get our parents to come pick us up. During our walk back to the clubhouse, Alex offered me a cigarette. It was the first and only cigarette of my life. It was awful. After choking on some fumes from my attempt to smoke, we started walking back when Alex offered his opinion of my play.

"Trevor, you golf like a fag."

One short sentence had me reconsidering my plan to come out. It wasn't the first time he'd insinuated or outright mocked me because he thought I was gay, but it was different this time. There wasn't anyone to impress this time, he used those words without thinking. Demeaning each other and calling each other gay around the team was frustrating, but it was a fact of teenage athletic life at the time. We would all use those words without thinking, and they didn't always have a deeper hurtful intention behind them. Saying it in the privacy of our walk back to the clubhouse seemed to confirm his biases against queer people. I said nothing.

Once we got back to the clubhouse area Alex called his mother for a ride. We made ourselves comfortable at a picnic table and waited for his mom to come get us. There wasn't much left to say at that point. We had talked about the team and playing in fall baseball leagues to get better for the real season in the spring. Even though I was scared of the outcome, I chose to follow through with my plan to come out. I was sitting next to a guy who called me a fag, who I planned to tell I was gay. A guy with three golf clubs in easy reach.

"You said earlier I golf like a fag. That's probably because I am one. I'm gay."

At the time, I thought I was having an out of body experience where time slows down, because the words seemed to be coming out of my mouth very slowly. I thought that the anxiety and stress of the moment would make me say everything in a rush and that I wouldn't be understood. Later that day Alex would tell me that it wasn't an illusion, I actually had slowed down my enunciation of each word for some reason. After getting the words out, I braced myself for whatever ridicule or hate he would throw at me. Proving the adage that you shouldn't judge a book by its cover correct, his response was not at all what I expected.

He fell off the picnic table. Yes, Alex is my furniture faller. With the benefit of hindsight, I can admit that my fears about coming out to him were overblown. In the moment, I was convinced that my life was going to change significantly and probably not for the better. In a lot of ways, my life did change, but not in the way I thought they would. Alex had many questions that afternoon. Questions I answered in between his supplications to God about why all the gays he knew kept coming out to him. I tried to answer as many questions as I could and suggested that perhaps people come out to him because we trust him. Saying that out loud made me realize that I must have trusted him on some level. I knew other people on the team for longer and was friendlier with them. They would have made more sense to come out to, but I chose Alex.

Alex and I both changed that afternoon. He apologized for past comments and said he'd speak up for me if the other guys on the team said anything out of line. The next two seasons of baseball he was true to his word and kept a lid on the casual homophobia on the team. It wasn't long before that kind of language was completely stamped out, largely due to his influence and unwillingness to let people say the things they used to say. I grew from the encounter as well. I started trusting in the people around me and came out to more of my teammates, and then to the wider community around me. I learned a lot about not prejudging people and believing that people could accept me for my genuine self.

I haven't seen Alex in years, but I take the memory of our golf game with me as a reminder to see people in a better light than my other instincts want me to believe. That lesson serves me well in all aspects of my life, and it's a lesson I might not have learned if I hadn't taken a chance on Alex and done some growing up of my own.

To Find Community

Written By Edward Borek

By the end of 2019, life had become stale, and I was looking for a change. After two years of reeling then rebuilding from a botched relationship, I had learned to embrace change. I had just turned 30, and I was building a brand new me! Why not a change of career, too, I thought.

I had been working in the same field for half my life by then. The work was monotonous, the people drab, and every day was the same as the one before it: wake up, work out, spend the rest of the day doing… I couldn't tell you what. Evening came, and at work I would take the same orders from the same regulars, then go to the same bar afterwards to drink the same drinks with the same people who told the same stories. Over and over again.

Yes, I needed a change. So, I enrolled in some online courses through an all-expense paid education program my employer offered for those looking to advance in the company. Should I have felt guilty that I didn't plan on staying with the business long term?

Brzzz—brzzz.

I looked down at my phone through blurred and bloodshot eyes.

Schedule update:

Double-shift added. Opening-9:30 AM.

Nope—the guilty feeling slipped away as I motioned for another shot.

In mid-March, the world shut down in response to a new and highly infectious virus. With little else to do, I threw myself into my studies. No more regulars; no more barflies. "Finally, a break from the monotony," I thought. But as the days turned to weeks and the weeks turned to months, I became listless. Like everyone else around the world, I was now in an intimate relationship with monotony. Social distancing measures meant everyone had to stay home and away from others. I live alone, which didn't make the social isolation any easier.

Each morning, I would run through the park in my San Diego suburban neighborhood dodging masked walkers like something out of an end-of-days movie but Real Housewives-style. After, I would shower, eat breakfast, then sit down in my newly-fashioned stay-at-home office—my dining room—to work on my assignments. The classes were asynchronous and obviously conceived before the world knew what virtual college in a modern pandemic would look like. There were no Zoom lectures, Google Hangouts, or Facetime study breaks with classmates. The courses weren't self-paced or anything, but there was minimal peer interaction. It was an out-of-state school, too, so my unseen, unnamed cohort weren't even in the same time zone as me! The gnawing loneliness of the pandemic grew day by day.

By summer, the pandemic looked as though it was ending; things were getting better. Case counts were dropping, and restrictions and stay-at-home orders were being lifted. I prepared to return to work after a three-month furlough. Then it happened. The virus started spreading unchecked again. We now call it the summer surge—the first of many surges to come. The reopening plans screeched to a halt. Stay at-home orders and mask mandates were reimposed. People started stockpiling goods again; it was like we were starting all over.

I wasn't going back to work… if ever, I found out. With no chance of reopening, my company rescinded my furlough; I was laid-off. I lost my job, my health insurance, my sense of security, and my education benefit all with one phone call. But not my drive. Undeterred, I began the application process for a local community college.

Despite the pandemic, I was able to keep my education plan on track. But I was still longing for social interactions. Most of my connections moved to texting only, which is not a suitable replacement for IRL conversations. After my last long-term relationship ended, I took it pretty hard. I had been single for a few years by that point, and I decided it was time to put myself out there again, even if just to make new friends. You don't realize how much of your social life revolves around coworkers until you don't have any. COVID-19 put an end to any practical means of meeting new people, and living alone during a pandemic, during which seeing friends anyway other than through a screen was forbidden, was incredibly isolating. I saw transferring to a local school as a way to expand my social connections. Zoom friends were better than no friends after all.

I was nervous but excited.

Fresh meat. That's one way to describe freshman. Typically, they're lost in the sauce and have no idea what's going on or even how to get around campus. That last part didn't matter anymore; but during the first few days of the fall semester, I attended all the virtual orientations I could. I was returning to college as a 30-year-old, and I hadn't had the most traditional education growing up. Everything was new to me. But unlike most incoming college students, I was used to unconventional learning. I didn't feel hamstringed by the virtual nature of a pandemic-education, rather I found it useful for doing all the things—literally, I signed up for all of the extracurriculars I could. I craved community. So, when I learned of the list of student organizations the college offered, I was champing at the bit. I emailed several advisors, one of whom was for Club Spectrum, the college's LGBTQ+ student organization.

I identify as a bisexual, cisgender male, but I have never had many gay friends. When my ex and I ended things a few years back, much of my ties to that community also ended. My gay friends were really his friends. When I saw the college had a club for people like me, I thought, I could make some connections with a tribe I had always wanted to be a part of but never felt able or welcomed to.

Consequently, finding community is difficult when you're not in with the out group. As weird as that is to think about, it felt as though I was being rejected by other gay people.

I once read a line from a book called Zami: A New Spelling of My Name that read "…it was hard for me to believe that my being an outsider had anything to do with being a lesbian… [it] had everything to do with being Black." Now, I'm neither a lesbian nor black, but I can relate to feeling excluded by the LGBTQ community—feeling like I'm not queer enough to fit in. For Audre Lorde, it was not being white enough. As Lorde sought to do, I wanted to change that part of my life. I wanted to fit in; I wanted to be accepted.

So, I reached out. I attended a virtual meeting with several others, and I thought, "Ok, yeah—this could be a good thing." Then at the following meeting, besides myself, only one other student showed up. The others, from the first Zoom, were former students coming to say hi to the handful of college staff and faculty who had attended, or so I came to find out.

Suffice to say, I was a little let down finding the club not to be what I had hoped. I came looking to find a group that I had imagined but that just wasn't there. However, community isn't about how many individuals are gathered together, it's about acceptance. I felt accepted, seen and validated in those first couple meetings.

After that, I threw all my effort into creating a space I had wanted to find. Even if it was just going to be me and one other student, I was determined to find that community. I couldn't have known at the time that I was building the space others would eventually seek out just as I had. I got to work and asked my friends and spammed my classes looking for new members. Anything to get the word out. I worked with the advisor on ways to find students and how to engage with them. I visited other clubs and attended student government meetings talking up Club Spectrum. I used my web and graphic design skills to create a comprehensive website for the club. I poured hours into it. I kept thinking up ways to connect people.

One by one, more students joined our meetings. We created art and writings about historical LGBTQ individuals and had virtual game nights. We helped others in video-chat study groups and volunteered our time to distribute food to the needy on campus, and we mobilized to plan a resource fair for LGBTQ+ individuals. Word was spreading and a community was taking shape. As Lorde puts it, the whole idea is that you need a place, even if it isn't what you thought you needed.

Today, I lead an organization that attracts students who, like me before, were looking for community. "For some of us there was no one particular place, and we grabbed whatever we could from wherever we found space, comfort, quiet, a smile, non-judgment." I found my people, and together we created the thing we all needed, whatever it looked like for each of us: volunteering, studying, gaming, writing, or web design. Community isn't just something you find, virtually or otherwise. And that's because, to find community, you have to build community.

Ugly Duck
Written By Colter Long

I played with Barbies instead of trucks, I liked to dress up in my babysitter's dresses, I loved to dance, and, because of those things, I was relentlessly bullied in school. When puberty hit, I began noticing how tight cowboys wore their Wrangler jeans. I lived half of my life in fear and shame. Keeping my secret seemed to be my only option. Gay people only existed in TV shows like Will & Grace, not in my hometown! I wasn't going to be the first person in my school to come out. Besides, I couldn't be sure until I at least *tried* to be straight to be sure I wasn't. I believed life would be so much easier if I could just find the right girl and then I wouldn't be haunted by the crushes I had on boys.

My parents were typical prairie people that moved to Alberta from Ontario because they loved the open fields and expansive horizons. Mom had calloused hands from sorting mail all day at our little town's post office and dad was a long-haul truck driver. I know some kids must dream of living on a big farm with horses, but I felt suffocated by the emptiness of the bald prairies. There were flies, and dirt, and mud, endless chores, and relentless boredom. I was an only child. No siblings to play with, fight with, defend, or be protected by. The taunting began every morning on the big yellow school bus and ended every day the same way. My first wrong move was bringing Barbie on board. From that day on, my fate was sealed. You see I was already an outsider because I was the only one on my bus route who wasn't related to everybody else. Begging my mom to enroll me into figure skating instead of hockey didn't help my situation either. "My dad says only boys play hockey, and only girls figure skate!" Announced one of the freckled gremlins in my first grade class. By this logic, I was now labelled as the "girly boy". I stood up for myself once and pushed the biggest, baddest bully away from me after he shouted insults in my face for the duration of our half-hour bus ride home. I struck him so hard his nose bled from both nostrils. He retaliated back by slamming my head into the stainless metal between the cracked vinyl bus seats giving me my first set of stitches.

It's bad enough to be called a girl in elementary class, but middle school is a whole new playing field. They began to call me GAY. The words GAY, HOMO, and FAG were thrown at me, along with stones, fists, and sometimes small change with seemingly raw hatred and disgust. I believed I was a good person; how could I be this "gay" abomination that is clearly unacceptable? My attraction to men became increasingly undeniable, but I promised myself I would never, ever act out on it. Not if doing so meant being labelled a freak that would be forever excluded from the cool crowd, or any crowd for that matter. I lived with pain-staking fear of rejection and believed that being accepted or loved was a privilege reserved for normal kids who didn't have to live with my secret.

Ricky Martin and Ben Affleck kept creeping into my thoughts nightly. I prayed that it was a phase. I tried to overcompensate those impulses by plastering pages from Maxim and Stuff magazines all over my bedroom wall. I thought my condition could be cured by getting a girlfriend. I begged every female in my grade seven class to go out with me. They all said no. I was even so desperate I paid a girl $10 to set me up with her friend long-distance in Prince George. I went out with one pixie-haired blonde from a neighbouring town for two weeks. She dumped me because she was taunted for dating the "ballerina boy". My first kiss belonged to another short-haired girl who was really interested in me, and this was far more terrifying than being single. I broke it off with her the day after her 16th birthday and explained that Pisces and Aquarius were a match that could never work.

Then I met her… Caitlin, a sophisticated city girl from Red Deer at a teen camp retreat. I walked into a rec room where she was entertaining a crowd of kids by playing "Fur Elise" on a piano. I don't understand how, but my emotional attachment compounded for her over the next three years. Every song reminded me of her, and I counted the minutes until I would talk to her on the phone. I thought about her all day... Except of course for the last three minutes of the day when I thought about Ben Affleck.

Caitlin was my high school graduation date. She looked elegant at the ceremony in a black and white polka-dot dress and a pearl necklace she borrowed from her grandma. Two hours later we were bussed out to a muddy baseball diamond and got lit off cans of Smirnoff Ice. Her dad came to pick her up the next morning. Oddly enough, her parents never seemed to be threatened by me and let her stay out with me as long as we wanted.

In the course of our intimate affair, I never made it past first-base with Caitlin, and nor did I try. Caitlin and I separated while she studied abroad in Germany for a year. During this time, I graduated high school and a week later I moved to Calgary. In 2004, on the night the Flames lost the Stanley Cup, I scored with the coolest, most beautiful girl I had ever met – like Regina George cool. To be honest, thinking about all the big shirtless hockey fans I had just seen out on the Red Mile is what got me through the whole awkward experience. If any woman could make a gay man straight, it was this girl. The problem was, she didn't.

One of my first jobs in the city was at a Banana Republic. I wasn't sure, but I thought some of these retail guys might be… you know… that way. They all stared at me a certain way and smirked when I professed my straightness. I explained that I had a girlfriend overseas and that there was this girl I had sex with, more than once even! Our first staff outing led to my own personal outing. We went to the local gay bar "Twisted Element" just a few blocks from my apartment. It was a birthday, and it would have been rude of me not to attend. Besides, I'd always been kind of curious about what these gays get up to. It would be something to check off on my big-city-to-do list. I didn't know what to expect. I spent the first hour or so confessing my attraction to women. Generally, the guy would give me that funny smile and be on his way. I'd just say, "Oh, no. I'm actually straight, people just think that because I'm a dancer."

Then one guy said, "Uh no, you're not."

What?! He must not have heard me correctly, "No really, I'm straight dude."

"No, you're not. It's okay. I just came out this month. It's not a big deal, just accept it."

My heart sank. I recalled a Dr. Phil episode I had seen the week before about gay husbands. Dr. Phil said, "If it quacks like a duck, walks like a duck, and hangs out with other ducks in the duck pond, it's a duck."

Oh fuck, I was a duck. There I was at the duck pond, surrounded by other duck and quacking. It hit me like a drag queen's rhinestone-studded clutch to the face. I was gay! I didn't want to grow up, live a lie, marry a woman only to someday divorce her and end up coming out on a daytime talk show in my mid-40s. I went home and laid on my bed in the fetal position for two days. I spilled my heart onto the pages of my journal and called my best friend from back home. I think she had been expecting this call for a long time.

"I have something to tell you…" I dramatically told my clique of small-town girlfriends in their college townhouse. They knew of course, they'd always known. It was apparently only a surprise to me, and that one girl I had slept with. My life hadn't ended! It had only just begun. I could finally be honest with myself. I wrote about real feelings, I had real conversations, and my friendships became authentic. I began to look people in the eyes when I spoke. Being in the closet was like living life behind a veil, always filtering my words, and always trying to adopt a more “masculine” tone of voice or posture so I wouldn't get “caught”.

My first visit to my friends back home was nerve-racking. The girls back home were concerned with if their blue-collar boyfriends home from the oil rigs would be able to accept me. They'd never met a real live gay person in the flesh. It was tense at first, but two beers later and I was sitting on the laps of these self-proclaimed rednecks and taking photos with them. If you're gay and have had the pleasure of being in Alberta, you've heard it before, "Hey dude, you know… I wasn't sure what to make of you, but you're a pretty cool guy. Like I'm not that way or anything, but I got your back. If anyone has a problem with you, I'll knock 'em out. I'm totally comfortable with my sexuality and all. I'm not gay or hitting on you. But you know, if I was, I would... It's all good man."

Now how was Caitlin going to take the news? I waited with her family at the airport for her when she landed home from Germany. She left a princess in pearls and returned with dreadlocks and tattoos. I barely recognized her. We got back to her place, sat on her bed, and at the same time blurted, "I have something to tell you." She told me she had fallen in love (for real) with a guy, and I told her I was also sleeping with men. We hugged, chuckled, and she barely flinched at the thought of me being gay. Our relationship evolved as we began to party and take home boys together. Looking back, my feelings for her at the time were genuine. Even though I wasn't sexually attracted to her, I fell in love with her intelligence, sense of humour, and charm – the same qualities I now look for on dates with men.

Now that word was beginning to spread, it was time to tell my parents before they heard it through the grapevine. My hometown of Stettler only has a population of 5,000 and good news travels faster than lightning. I was walking with my mom in Cowtown Calgary past the street the gay bar was on. I told her that the club I went to was over there and that it was great, because I didn't have to spend money on a cab home, it was so close.

"What's the name of it," she asked. "Twisted Element," I said nonchalantly.

She dropped her mouth and gasped, "I know what that place is!"

"How do you know? I didn't even know until a few months ago." My face must have gone three shades of red from shock.

"Don't you get guys hitting on you?" Her voice went up an octave as she shook her head and wrinkled her nose.

"I guess you get what you put out," I grinned nervously.

"Don't you like girls anymore?" She stopped and turned to me.

I paused for an awkward moment, "No, I guess I don't... Don't tell me you didn't already know?"

She chuckled, "Well, I wouldn't say I did, but a co-worker seemed to think she knew." The tension gradually subsided after our ritualistic day at the mall. Later in the food court, she added, "I got a family full of fruit loops, and you're the biggest one of the bunch!" I think it was her way of saying that we all have our eccentricities and that's what makes us special. We laughed it off and life went on as normal. Surprisingly to me, she was more in disbelief that people didn't wait outside the gay bar to harass patrons. She didn't care what I did as long as I was safe and happy.

I told my dad a year later when we were all fighting about something totally unrelated, and I thought I might as well do it while tensions were already high. He didn't understand at first, but he has made it very clear that he supports my happiness 100%.

I changed my status on Nexopia from "straight" to "bi-curious". It was on the internet and official now. I was ready to go back to Twisted

Element! I'd been waiting 20 years for this moment. I was going to get with a man, I was going to meet the boyfriend of my dreams, he was going to love me, and we were going to live happily ever after. All the shit I had been through was about to turn to gold. I spotted him smiling at me. Tanned skin, big almond eyes, and wearing an argyle driver's cap probably bought at Le Chateau. I summoned enough liquid courage to casually "bump" into him.

"Hello, I've just come out of the closet. Would you like to be my first kiss with a guy?"

He responded enthusiastically and we kissed. I was excited to finally be in the game that I had previously only been a spectator. I had watched all of my straight friends navigate the highs and lows of dating and it was now my time to experience it. Since then, I have been in love and had my heart broken a few times – every time I grow a little bit more and develop a better relationship with myself.

It's hard to believe there was a time when I prayed to be straight because now, I wouldn't change being gay for anything. The loneliness I felt from being a misfit in a country town gave me the sense that there must be something more that I was missing. Where others may not have had a reason to leave, I left in search of acceptance, adventure, and love. I didn't find all of those things right away, but I eventually found a community of

LGBTQ people that have become my chosen family. Today, I am educated, I have a meaningful career, live in a city that feels like home, and I have authentic relationships with people who love me for me.

I later that one of my best friends in high school was gay too but he was too afraid to tell me because he thought I would judge him. It's sad to think we were both dealing with our sexuality alone and could have supported one another if the stigma about being gay wasn't so shaming. I've come to learn now that there were many of us in my small town who didn't come out because we had no role models or examples of how to do it. For me, coming out was quite a dramatic process because it was rare to find gay people. Now there is a Gay-Straight Alliance at my old school and last summer there was a Pride float in my town's annual parade. In the future, we may still need to come out but with more acceptance, my hope is that it will be less of a declaration and more like sharing your preference for soft drinks – I've tried both Cola and Sprite and now I just stick with Cola.

Who Speaks for Us?
Written By Stephen Parnes

Who says it's all about pride?
For some, we are destined to hide. So, where is our pride?
And who is our guide?

Please, think before you speak. We're not all settled on the creek*.
Keep us in mind as you choose to unwind, We're not freaks; we just want life to be kind.

How about considering what we need? We also deserve to be freed.
When October comes to town, Don't cast a dark frown,

Be thoughtful, be sensitive, and look around.

We're not all full of pride, Our world has trouble inside, I hope you can reach out,
Be more receptive, even cast doubt.

Be more than a day of pride,
Act and recognize that there is more inside.

A day of pride should be about all of us, It's not—such a fuss,
Exclusive of all who swim against the tide, Please, folx, consider our side.

Oh, how much feeling is deep inside.
Lord, oh, Lord, who speaks for us, my side?

ACT II: ALONE OR LONELY

Twinks and tweens, in shorts and jeans,
I wonder if they truly comprehend what all of this means.

On the creek*, all alone,
Acting busy, peering at my phone: The time, the temp, nothing more,
Who gives a damn about a baseball score?

Twinks and teens, jeans and queens, Politicians and college deans.

I wish for more, oh, so much more, Where's my man, be he rich or poor?

Alphabet of Hope

Oh, how much emotion is deep inside. Lord, oh,
Lord, who speaks for us, my side?

Who Are We in This World?

Written By Stephen Parnes

Pride Celebrations? Rainbow and ally flags? Automobile bumper stickers proclaiming equality and same-sex Subarus?

What about the rest of us? The closeted, fearful, shunned, and simply those afraid of our own skins, feelings, and hopes & dreams?

Do you know how debilitating an absence of love, of desire for a family and “normal life” can be? I do. I live it every single day … and every single night alone in bed, in a house devoid of chatter and laughter and joy.

We're here. We're queer. But we don't celebrate and acclaim. We keep to ourselves, have silent confidants, and socialize in "mysterious ways."

Yup. We're not a rarity. We're not so alone. But, let it be known, many of us are lonely, captive to our own fears and fences.

How I wish that I could be "normal," and by that I mean not only heterosexual but even outwardly gay and free. I'm not. I don't enjoy the spirit and affection and boisterous display of so many others, both straight and gay.

Why is "Pride" a supposed feeling for all of us? I, for one, don't feel pride, and I doubt that I'm alone. Why is recognition for the fearful, afraid, awkward, and ambivalent not addressed? Why is it a celebration … or, otherwise, complete submission and sadness and a sense of personal failure? Where is our symbol, our day, our simple acceptance and note? Why do we feel abandoned, ostracized, and even discarded in a "gay world" rejoicing and abuzz in color and openness and flamboyance?

Yes, I'm gay and sadly alone. Lonely even too often.

Why is the "gay culture" so narrow in focus, so discriminating like other social entities, so emboldened that it forgets the many forgotten? It's time for a change, for bolder and grander and broader recognition. It's time for "gay culture" to accept and recognize, support, and care for all of us, all of us who don't walk the same line as others.

Meet Hope Pages Press Ltd.

Trevor Ritchie is the CEO and co-founder of Hope Pages Press Ltd, an international printing imprint focused on bringing forward the stories of marginalized groups in society. Trevor lives, works and sometimes plays on the unceded territories of the Coast Salish Peoples. Outside of Hope Pages Press, Trevor is a teacher in the Burnaby School District, and was one of the proponents of SOGI policy development in Burnaby Schools. Trevor also works as a sports ambassador for the Canadian Olympic Team's OneTeam program. Trevor works to explore the ability of athletics to be affirming to LGBTQ+ people.

Michael Arendt is a co-founder and editor-in-chief of Hope Pages Press Ltd. While he is sad that he wasn't able to contribute a story to this anthology, he enjoyed both editing the stories and creating the design of Alphabet of Hope. He hopes to be able to contribute to future editions of the anthology. Michael is an alumnus of Wayne State University where he earned a Bachelor of Arts in Design & Merchandising. Aside from Hope Pages Press Ltd, Michael teaches dance classes and does freelance design work. He would like to thank his husband, Paul, for supporting him on the endeavor of starting a publishing imprint and publishing

Alphabet of Hope. He'd also love to give many thanks to Trevor Ritchie for allowing Michael to partner with him on this journey.

Meet The Authors

Edward Borek, or Edward J. Borek III knows how important finding affirming spaces is for disproportionately impacted individuals. In his short story, "To Find Community," he explores what it takes to build such a community for LGBTQ+ college students. Edward is a long-time volunteer, an effective student leader, and community advocate. Learn more at www.edwardborek.com.

Kellen Bunting- A graduate of Salem State, Kellen lives in Boston, Massachusetts. Adopted early in life, he makes greater efforts to appreciate his privileges and life luck than he ever could have envisioned as a child.

Lillith Campos is the parent of 4 beautiful children that she adores. She volunteers her time facilitating trans support groups and provides safe zone trainings to promote inclusivity with various organizations. She practices intersectional feminism and advocates for equality with a passion for mental health awareness and suicide prevention. www.onslowcountylgbtq.com

Parker Chapple can be found at parker@badasscreative.ca

Monica Furlotte appreciates art in any format; often attending poetry events, art galleries, concerts, and plays. Over the last few years, she started being involved in art projects herself to raise awareness on different issues she is passionate about & as a form of self-expression. Music is her love language.

Brett Grunerud is a current PharmD student at the University of British Columbia in beautiful Vancouver, British Columbia. Apart from school and work at a pharmacy on weekends, Brett enjoys curling in the winter and volunteering with a variety of community and university-based organizations.

Austin Johnson is a licensed clinical social worker (aka brain fixer upper) who lives with his husband and coven of witches in Salem, Oregon. When not benevolently manipulating people, he enjoys finding random uses for discarded bits and rationalizing his perpetually messy workspace as "part of the creative process."

Alex Keen- A writer, an award-winning improv comedian and a designer of TTRPGs, Alex Keen lives in Sheffield, England with his partner and no pets or children, thank you. Find his work at www.alexrkeen.com.

Colter Long grew up on a fam outside of Stettler, Alberta. As a teenager, he was diagnosed with Leukemia and was the recipient of a bone marrow transplant. This experience influenced his interest in the biopsychosocial aspects of wellness. Colter is now is a practicing clinical therapist in Vancouver, British Columbia. Colter can be found at https://www.linkedin.com/in/colter-j-long/

Alex Masse, AKA Fairything, is a 21-year-old writer and musician residing in what is colonially known as Surrey, BC. The arts are a longtime love of theirs, and their work has been seen everywhere from the Scholastic Writing Awards to Vancouver Pride. They're also a neurodivergent nonbinary lesbian, which greatly affects their process.

McRae (All Pronouns) is a neurodiverse writer and creator. He seeks to use his art to challenge the status quo, inspire independent and critical thinking, and inspire and amplify the voices of the marginalized. He'd like to thank the Squamish Nation for putting up with him and his strange family for over a century on their unceded territory.

Conner Mertens- In 2014, Conner Mertens became the first active college football player to ever come out publicly about his sexuality. Since then, he has been involved with groups like GLSEN, PFLAG, The Human Rights Campaign, and many more. In addition, he serves on an advisory board for The Trevor Project, is co-chair for the You Can Play Project on the West coast and directs the Sports Equality Foundation's youth advisory committee.

Stephen Parnes can be found at sparnesncs@hotmail.com

Micah Porter has been a public educator for three decades as a teacher, coach, LGBTQ+ advocate, and administrator. He has a deep philosophical belief in creating greater educational access for our most under-resourced students and creating positive experiences, both academic and extracurricular. His advocacy focuses on greater inclusion for LGBTQ+ teen athletes. Having worked with the Sports Equality Foundation, You Can Play, and Teens for Inclusive Athletics, among others, Micah has been a committed spokesperson in the LGBTQ+ sports movement.

James Sanyshyn is a Burnaby teacher. His Alberta upbringing fed his mission for equity and inclusion in the world of education. He was one of the main proponents of SOGI policy development in Burnaby schools. He is graduate of UBC and McGill University, trained in music and French.

David J.C. Smith has recently completed his Masters in Sport and Exercise psychology at the German Sports University of Cologne, following a Bachelor of Science on Sport and Exercise Science at Metropolitan State University of Denver. Over the last twelve years he has worked with the LGBTQI community in promoting exercise, fitness and sport as well as teaching, lectures, workshops and seminars/webinars in sport psychology, sports science, and sports diversity. David came out when he was 14 and spent his formative years working in the amusement park industry, an experience from which his story derives.

Derek Smith lives in Vancouver, Canada. Educated at the University of British Columbia with a MSc in Chemistry, he worked in academia and private industry until 2020. Derek has since left that career to focus on his passion of skydiving and is now working as a professional skydiver.

PAGES PRESS LTD.

Alphabet of Hope is just the beginning of the story at Hope Pages Press Ltd. If you have a short story, fiction or non-fiction, or a novel, significantly featuring LGBTQ+ characters, please submit your work for consideration at contact@hopepagespress.com

Manufactured by Amazon.ca
Bolton, ON

26020757R00105